TIPS FOR THE *Traveling* QUILTER

TIPS FOR THE *Traveling* QUILTER

Your adventure guide for visiting quilt shows, retreats, shop hops, quilt cruises — and more!

FIRST EDITION

RONA HERMAN

PUBLISHED BY RONA THE RIBBITER, LLC

Published by Rona the Ribbiter, LLC. 6925 Medlin Road, Monroe, NC 28112, www.RonatheRibbiter.com

ISBN: 978-1-7371605-0-2 • 978-1-7371605-1-9

Printed in the United States. 1st Printing.

Credits: Designed by: Lindsie Bergevin. Edited by: Kathy Cornwell.

DEDICATION

To Mom, for inspiring my love for travel adventures of every sort.

To Arianna, for launching me into the amazing world of quilting.

To Stefan, for always supporting my crazy ideas of mashing the two together.

CONTENTS

WILD ATLANTIC WAY, IRELAND

CHAPTER ONE

Do Quilter's Really Travel?

INTRODUCTION

I believe all things happen for a reason. Including pandemics.

When I started my *Rona the Ribbiter* blog back in 2018, I thought I was going to be the next best quilt pattern designer. I was going to spend all day creating patterns, writing posts about quilting, teaching quilting, and writing pattern books about quilting. You know, just like the thousands of other amazing quilt bloggers out there. My, how things change.

By early 2020, I was neck-deep in writing my first quilt book. Each quilt was inspired by the quilt tour I took to Ireland in 2017. The quilts were nearly finished; the travel reservations for my second trip to Ireland were made. I was going to spend the entire month of May in Ireland, taking photographs and putting the finishing touches on my first quilting book.

Then, COVID closed the world.

By the end of March, it became clear that the entire world was shutting its doors. The United States closed its borders to any non-citizen and to non-essential travel. Then Ireland closed its borders as well. It was official: My trip, and my book, was placed on a permanent hold.

Like a splash of ice water after a hot shower, our entire world changed. In the blink of an eye, quilt shows were canceled, quilt shops closed their doors, and the world seemed to stop moving.

I'll be honest: I cried. I literally went through a mourning period of at least a few months, trying

ME WHEN I FOUND OUT MY TRIP TO IRELAND WAS CANCELLED

to figure out if all the time and energy I'd poured into the book had been wasted. Months of being engulfed with nothing but Ireland was all gone. Like so many people around the country who got furloughed or even lost their job altogether, I asked myself, "What do I do now?" And like many children do when faced with tremendous uncertainty, I went home to see my mother.

Every June, I fly to Nevada to visit my parents. My mother's birthday almost always falls right in between the Quilt Show Reno and Father's Day. So it's usually a no-brainer trip. As you can imagine, 2020 proved a little different. There was no quilt show. And the Reno Rodeo (Mom's favorite June event) was also canceled. So I decided to pack our bags and take my mother to Las Vegas.

About this same time, with the help of Zoom, the world slowly started to change its trajectory. Quilt guilds began meeting online. Museums began showcasing their collections online. Quilt marketers created the "Virtual Quilt Show" and quilt shops around the globe began slowly reopening their doors. We made thousands of masks and an untold number of people pulled out their sewing machines for the first time in years or perhaps decades. For the first time in months, there was hope on the horizon.

The Vegas trip was very short, only a weekend getaway, but we had so much fun! And of course I blogged about it the entire time. I wrote up tips on how to travel down from Reno to Vegas; how to travel during COVID, how Las Vegas was "staying safe," and much more. It felt like the ideas (and travel tips) were flowing from an unending spring, and my audience began to grow.

I heard from so many of you, asking questions and sharing stories about all sorts of quilting travel, including trips

QUILT SHOW RENO

CAEASARS PALACE TREVI FOUNTAIN

40 SHADES OF GREEN QUILT IN WASHINGTON STATE

you'd made in the past and trips you were planning after the pandemic. Then it hit me. There really was no other place to find answers and details specifically about **quilting travel** all in one place. THIS is what my blog is truly about. So, THIS is what my first book should be about: all things quilting travel related!

I immediately got to work, writing down more ideas, sharing more stories, and putting them all together in this great one-stop-shop *Tips for the Traveling Quilter* handbook. In this book you get all of my best tips, suggestions, and a few of my travel shenanigan stories along the way. My hope is when you're ready to get back on the road, you can use this book to travel better, easier, and safer, as well as to inspire your next great quilting adventure!

Oh, and those Ireland quilts I mentioned? I've included two of the patterns for you at the end of this book. There's really no taking the designer out of the quilt book author.

DO QUILTERS REALLY TRAVEL THAT MUCH?

At last measure, quilting as a whole is a 4.2 billion dollar industry. Oh, yes: that's million with a 'B'. And even throughout the pandemic, that number has been steadily growing. Also, according to an early 2020 poll*, there are approximately 9-11 million quilters in the United States, and about 65% of whom are retired. Couple that with the following statistic: According to USTravel.org, "US residents logged 1.9 billion trips for leisure in 2019." I'm not sure about you, but those numbers astounded me.

Every year, states and countries all over the world put on quilt shows of various sizes, inviting travelers to visit their quilt shops and explore their regions.

**Quilting statistic results provided by quilting trends survey conducted by Premier Needle Arts, 2020*

Quilt groups of all shapes and sizes travel to quilt retreats in all corners of the United States and abroad. So it stands to reason that the quilting travel industry (post-COVID) will be continually on the rise as well. And I'll probably be leading the way. "Follow me to Fabric!" Ooh, that would make a great bumper sticker!

Over the last few months, I've been able to talk to hundreds, if not thousands, of quilters online. Everyone from quilting teachers and show vendors to the everyday quilter have expressed their concerns regarding travel because of the pandemic. That's why I've made sure to include an entire section dedicated to traveling post COVID. This mess can't last forever, right?

However, those same quilters have also expressed to me how much they can't wait to get back out on the road. I should mention that I will never try to tell someone to travel or not to travel. That is solely up to you and your personal comfort level. However, when you are ready, this book can give you the tools to make your quilting adventures great!

BUDGETING YOUR QUILTING TRAVEL ADVENTURE

One of the most common questions I get asked is how I can afford to travel so often. I suppose that depends on how you travel.

Advertisers like to make money. That's really no surprise to anyone. Unfortunately, those same advertisers charge so much that only the giant travel companies can afford to advertise with them. Therefore, the giant travel companies are the only ads most people see. It leaves a person with a skewed perception that travel is extremely expensive. This is not actually the case.

There are *travelers* and there are *vacationers.*

A *vacationer* is someone who saves money throughout the year to spend on one or perhaps two extravagant vacations. On these vacations, they'll stay at a nice hotel, eat every meal at nice restaurants, buy lots of souvenirs, and maybe even take in a show or two. Sounds wonderful, right? And expensive.

Conversely, the *traveler* tends to travel in similar ways to how they live at home. They've learned a few tips to save money here and there and are much more frugal in their travel habits. Basically, travelers put the most emphasis on the travel experience. This way, they can afford to go more places more often.

The bottom line is: No matter if you're traveling to a quilt show or on a shop hop road trip, we travelers know how to make a budget work its magic.

CREATING YOUR TRAVEL BUDGET

I am a list and numbers person. Seriously, you should see the number of notepads I go through in a month. Therefore, one of the travel highlights for me is creating a budget for each of my quilting trips. Sounds so exciting, doesn't it? However, knowing my budget ahead of time has helped me stay on track in many situations.

To get started creating your road travel budget, you'll need to know 5 main numbers: Lodging, Food, Travel, Miscellaneous, and FABRIC!

Lodging

I am a big proponent of using homestays. For the majority of my trips, I try to find a good one in the area. In most cases you can almost always find one cheaper than staying at a hotel chain. Plus, there are many other advantages to staying in a homestay, like having a place to spread out and sew at night, just to name one.

Recently, I was in Washington State visiting family and needed a place to stay on Whidbey Island. There are really no hotels on the south end of Whidbey Island. In fact, the closest hotel chains are a short ferry ride across the bay in Mukilteo. However, at $9 per trip to and from the island, it gets pretty expensive.

So I turned to one of the largest websites for homestays: AirBnB.com.

Luckily, I found the most amazing little house right on the water! The backyard was literally the beach. And the house was close enough to the Whidbey Island southern ferry dock that we got to watch the ferries come and go. The AirBnB.com homestay

AIRBNB IN MUKILTEO, WASHINGTON

WHIDBEY ISLAND FERRY SUNRISE

host provided everything we could have needed, including full bottles of shampoo and body wash in the shower and laundry soap in the laundry room. It was the perfect house. The cost? With taxes and fees, it worked out to a total of $196 per night.

Now, I can already hear the comments about how expensive that is. However, keep in mind this was a 3-bedroom house that slept 6 people. It had a full kitchen, bath, washer and dryer, and a working fireplace. Heck, for 6 people staying in a hotel you'd need at least 3 rooms. All that coupled with saving the money from going back and forth across the ferry to visit my family made the house rental incredibly affordable. And did I mention that view!?

To help give you a better idea of how to plan your quilting adventure budget, let's use my latest trip to the Blue Ridge Parkway in the North Carolina mountains as an example. Using a homestay lodging I was able to find a home to rent for around $70 per night. That worked out to be a total of $630 for 9 nights.

Food

According to travel expert Rick Steves, you should budget $30 per person per day for food costs. This includes eating breakfast at your hotel (or homestay), taking a lunch with you, and enjoying dinner out at the end of the day.

ANDREW JACKSON HOTEL, NEW ORLEANS

It's simple math really. If you go on a trip and eat out at every meal, the costs add up pretty quickly. So instead, I always plan to eat the majority of my meals at my lodging. Now, if you are staying at a homestay lodging with a kitchen, this is pretty easy. However, if you are staying in a hotel, this might not be so easy but it can be done.

On past trips, I've had to get pretty creative with my food plans. For instance, my favorite is the breakfast buffet spread at our New Orleans hotel. There was no fridge or microwave in our hotel room. But we did have a coffee maker (hot water), so I brought snacks, oatmeal, a few dry goods, paper plates, bowls, and plastic ware. With no real place for storage, I had them all laid out on a hotel towel on the floor. It wasn't pretty, but it worked!

With a little planning, and a fridge and/or microwave in your hotel room, you can easily have a variety of breakfasts, packed lunches, and snacks for the day all from your hotel.

Simply create a meal plan for each day before heading on your trip. Then, pack accordingly. Plus, you can always go grocery shopping along your route if needed. Luckily, on my trip to the NC Mountains, my homestay lodging was only a few minutes from a major grocery store.

As it was just me on the North Carolina mountains trip and I was going to be gone a total of 10 days, I budgeted $300 for food costs.

Travel

Depending on where you're traveling, your road trip travel budget costs can vary tremendously. If you are flying, this is where you would include your airfare cost. If you are driving, this is where you want to include gas costs and any potential car rental fees.

To figure out my approximate gas cost I take the total miles divided by my car's miles per gallon. This will give me the number of gallons I need. Then, multiply the number of gallons by the current price per gallon of gasoline.

By planning my North Carolina mountain trip route on an online map, I was able to estimate that my driving distance up and back would be approximately 600 miles total. I plugged that number into my gas mileage equation, and rounding up, found I would need at least $50 for gas.

Gas Budget

600 miles / 25 mpg
= 24 gallons

24 gallons x $2 / gal.
= $48.00

KEYCHAIN FROM GEORGIA

KEYCHAIN FROM NEW ORLEANS

KEYCHAIN FROM SEATTLE

Miscellaneous

Whenever you travel, there are bound to be some extra costs along the way. Personally, I LOVE going through antique shops and usually find at least one or two items begging to come home with me.

For instance, I collect key rings. At every place I've traveled to over the years, I've picked up one or the other, or both. That, plus the occasional t-shirt and souvenirs can blow any budget in a heartbeat. That's why I make sure to allow enough cushion for the "just in case" spending.

The Miscellaneous section is also where you want to include things like entrance fees for museums and parks, etc. I've found that using a round number of $25 per person per day usually fits about right.

For my 10-day trip to the North Carolina mountains, I budgeted $250 for all the miscellaneous spending.

Everyone's Favorite... Fabric!

Let's face it: We're going to buy fabric. And by "fabric" I'm referring to not just the cotton goodness itself, but also any and all gadgets and notion goodies we can find to help us turn that cotton goodness into quilts. Whether we're headed on a big shop hop road trip or to a quilt show, fabric is going to find its way into our bags. So that's why I made it its own category.

Because I visit a lot of quilt shops on the road, I try to limit myself. I'm sure you know how easy it is to go overboard on fabric, am I right? It's just so soft and pretty!! However, I've found I can usually stick to $25 per quilt shop.

Realistically, you're not going to spend exactly $25 at each quilt shop. At some, you may spend a little more. At others, you may spend a little less. It just all depends on the quilt shop. However, it usually evens out in the end. Of course, you can always increase this number (or decrease it) as you see fit.

For the North Carolina mountains road trip, I was going to visit 5 quilt shops, so my fabric budget was $125.

THE BREAKDOWN

With all the numbers in place, here's how my North Carolina mountains road trip budget shaped up:

So, how did I do?

I'd say I did pretty darn good, considering my spending actually came in at $100 under budget! Honestly, I was just as shocked as you.

✈ **PRO TIP:** *If you're headed to a quilt show, you can still use this same budgeting list for your trip. However, if you're like me and love a good quilt class, I would suggest adding a 6th section to your quilt show budget for "Classes." In this section, you'll add not only the cost of the class(es), but also any additional kit fees.*

BLOWING ROCK, NORTH CAROLINA

HOW DO I STAY ON BUDGET?

Here's the crux of the issue: Creating a budget is one thing. Sticking to that quilting travel adventure budget can be quite another. I can already hear the fabric calling my name! Even with the best of intentions, overspending is a real thing. So, here are a few tips I use to help me stay on budget.

Entertainment

One of the items I always include in my travel budget is the cost of entrance fees to museums and other miscellaneous adventures. However, this one can be hard to calculate if you don't know ahead of time the places you plan to visit. So I make it a point ahead of time to check online for places in the area I really want to see. Then I make a list of their importance.

HICKORY RIDGE MUSEUM IN BOONE, NORTH CAROLINA

For example, on that same North Carolina mountain trip, I knew I really wanted to see the Blowing Rock scenic area, Hickory Ridge History Museum, and the Mystery Hill area. However, my road trip budget did not accommodate all three of the things I wanted to see/do. So I decided Mystery Hill was the least important of the three and I could live without it.

Fabric

As I've mentioned, fabric is usually the hardest budget item to stick with, whether you're on a shop hop road trip, at a quilt show, or even on a quilt tour. However, I have a plan. No, really that's it: **Have a plan.** When you go in with a specific project or pattern in mind, instead of just looking around and being distracted by all the pretty things (like we all do anyway), your mind is more focused on filling an actual need.

If you don't already have a pattern in mind, make this your first purchase. At the first quilt shop (or vendor booth), your goal is to find your next favorite project pattern. Maybe it's a fabulous quilt. Maybe it's an amazing travel bag. I usually go with the travel bag. It's really become a bag pattern addiction at this point.

At the next quilt shop (or vendor booth), your goal may be to find the perfect fabric for that pattern. Stop #3: It's time to get those notions! And maybe a new gadget to aid in your project completion.

On my North Carolina mountains trip, I knew there were a few bags I wanted to make and one specific quilt project I needed fabric for. I decided I would choose one project for each of the 5 quilt shops I visited, so I could keep my shopping eye focused.

TIPS TO CUT COSTS ON THE ROAD

Everyone likes to save money. I know I do. But when it comes to quilting travel, all that fabric and those notions and gadgets can be a bit overwhelming. Especially when they're calling your name. Seemingly screaming it from across the room in some cases. So how do we combat those screams and stay on budget?

Travel in Groups

My number one favorite way to travel is definitely with my fellow quilters. It's really a win/win for everyone. When you share a car and lodging you can split the costs, which makes it more affordable for all of you. Plus, if everyone is amenable, you can also share the cooking duties. I love seeing what creative meals my friends come up with on the road!

Use a Travel Credit Card

** Before I go any further, I must make it clear that I am NOT an accountant nor do I endorse any specific credit card brand.*

This little trick was first mentioned to me by my accountant. He told me that when you do a lot of traveling, it actually pays to use an airline or hotel credit card to accumulate their points. If the card is used correctly, the points can add up quite quickly.

My home airport is Charlotte Douglas International, and it's a hub for American Airlines. Therefore, most of the flights I take in and out of the Charlotte airport are via American. Because of this, it made sense for me to get an American Airlines credit card that has a reward points program. This particular card also gives double points for purchases at grocery stores, gas stations, etc. So I pay for most things I would buy anyway (groceries, household bills) with that credit card to earn points toward a free flight.

Every year since I opened the airline credit card, I have earned enough points for at least one free roundtrip flight. In fact, I recently took a trip to see my mother in Nevada that was paid for entirely with points. Last year, I earned almost enough points for 2 free flights all by using the airline credit card for things I was going to spend money on anyway.

Just remember, the only way to actually save money using this trick is to keep the balance(s) paid down as you go so that you don't rack up those high interest fees. Therefore, if you already have high credit card balances, this may not be the right option for you.

Shop Around for Lodging

In all my travels, I have found that hotels can sometimes be the most expensive form of lodging. Not in every case, but many. That's why I like to shop around in the locations I know I'll be staying to find the best price and amenities.

As I mentioned previously, you can usually find some pretty great deals using AirBnB.com to find a homestay lodging. For example, I've found entire house rentals for as little as $50 per night.

If you're not yet familiar with AirBnB.com, they are a home share group that matches you with homeowners who have rooms, apartments, or entire homes for rent. You can rent them by the day or week, similar to a long-term stay hotel.

EPP BY FLASHLIGHT IN MUKILTEO, WASHINGTON

A few benefits to staying at a homestay lodging include the ability to cook meals "at home," room to spread out to work on quilt projects, and comfortable spaces to just relax on the couch and read a new quilt magazine.

Every time I travel to the West Coast, I find myself waking up at 4 AM because my body runs on East Coast time. Therefore,

I like to have that extra space at my homestay to work on projects or get some writing done before my day begins.

Also, AirBnB.com has lists of things to do and see in your travel area as well as coupons and other savings. Once I came across quilting classes being offered in Ireland!

✈ **PRO TIP:** *When booking a homestay using AirBnB.com, be sure to look for the ones marked "Superhost." These are hosts that have been fully vetted and guarantee their cleanliness, responsiveness, safety, and ease of renting. Also, make sure to check that the amenities you require are listed on the rental page and be sure to read all the reviews.*

✈ **BONUS TIP:** *Similar to the airline reward credit cards, most major hotel chains offer reward card programs as well. Each time you travel, you can earn points toward a free night's stay. My mother particularly likes this one because she is very partial to Holiday Inn Express hotels. If there is one nearby, that's where she'll stay. I chose to get a Hilton rewards credit card as they include several hotel chains to choose from depending on the destination. More options = more opportunity to earn points.*

Don't Be Afraid to Ask

Who doesn't love a good deal? Well, a little secret I have (ok, maybe it's not so secret) is to always ask the locals. This includes your rideshare driver, hotel staff, airport clerks, and especially the local quilt shop staff! You'll be amazed at what they might come up with.

FT LAUDERDALE, FLORIDA

Not that long ago, I spent my birthday in Florida with my sister. On our one free night in town, we asked the hotel's evening desk clerk what we should do. He pulled out a notebook full of coupons for local restaurants, bars, and entertainment places and started handing them to us. We ended up partying practically for free! Like I said, you just never know.

Plan to Eat In

As I mentioned previously, planning to "eat in" at your place of lodging can save tons of cash that could be better spent on, oh I don't know, MORE FABRIC!

But what kind of food should you take?

On my trips, I usually bring oatmeal, cereal, and some easy lunch items that will travel well. Each morning, I eat breakfast at my lodging and pack a lunch to take with me on my travels. By the end of the day, I'm usually too tired to cook, so I'll treat myself to a meal out. As long as you have a fridge in your hotel, or a full kitchen in your homestay lodging, you can easily plan to eat most of your meals from "home."

To save even more money, when you have a full kitchen at an extended stay or homestay lodging, plan a couple of "make ahead" meals and cook them on your first night there. Then, simply pack them in individual portions and stick them in the fridge. You can even do this at home before you leave and take the portions with you. Instead of eating out, you'll have a quick meal ready to be heated up.

Take Cash

As financial guru Dave Ramsey says, "Swiping plastic doesn't hurt like spending your hard-earned cash." And it's so true. When you can physically see the limited amount of money you have to spend, it forces you to be a bit pickier

BONUS TIP: A Few Good Sites

These are a couple of my favorite websites that I use when looking for travel deals. You can find coupons for hotels, airlines, car rentals, and more!

JoinHoney.com is a great app that I use quite often for many things, not just travel. When you go to any site online, Honey will automatically show you if there are any coupons available for use. They'll even watch items for you on Amazon and notify you if they find a price drop. I've already saved a ton using Honey!

Retailmenot.com is a great site for finding deals on everything from cash back offers to coupons on travel and even quilting supplies. I spotted one this morning for a great deal on a new fabric cutting machine!

Groupon.com is great for finding deals on just about anything you can imagine. And you can also search by location. So if you're going to be out on the road and want a massage or to find a great restaurant deal, just do a quick search!

about your purchases. Questions like "Do I NEED this or do I WANT this?" come to mind. I have had to implement this tactic at several quilt shows!

Leave Extra Room In the Budget

I'll be honest: I've definitely gone over my budget more than once. It's very easy to go overboard at a quilt show or quilt shop. This bad habit multiplies when you're visiting multiple quilt shops on a shop hop road trip. So, for this very reason, I always add a little extra cushion in the "Miscellaneous" portion of the budget. That way, if I do happen to go over a bit, I'm still covered. A good number would be to add 1 extra day of costs in your budget calculations.

TIPS FOR INTERNATIONAL TRAVEL

There are many reasons for international quilting travel. For instance, did you know that France, Spain, England, Australia, and Japan all host international quilt shows each year? Plus, there are tons of quilt tours that travel to nearly every continent. Or you could take an international trip on your own and stop at a few quilt shops, museums, etc. along the way.

No matter where you're headed, whether you're in a large group or solo, here are a few tips to help make your international trip a little smoother.

Buy Travel Insurance

Especially when traveling internationally, it's always a good idea to buy travel insurance. Think of all the things that can go wrong while on the road here at home. Now imagine them happening overseas. Will your current insurance(s) cover them?

Take medical problems. If you get sick, take a fall, or have a medical crisis in another country, even ones that may have a social health care program such as European and Scandinavian countries, that does not mean their national health care is available for non-citizens.

Luckily (knock wood), I have not had any major medical issues while traveling internationally. However, I know others that have. One person was in her 40's, traveling across Europe. She rented a bicycle for the day and ended up taking a bad fall and was rushed to the hospital. Because she had not opted to get travel insurance or to check with her insurance company prior to leaving the United States, she was forced to pay out of pocket for the entire cost.

Fortunately, all of the money she had set aside for the remainder of her trip was able to cover her medical bill. Unfortunately, that meant cutting her vacation short and heading home immediately. I don't even want to imagine what would have happened if she could not come up with the money.

For most of my trips, I like to use Allianz Travel insurance. Many travel companies also offer Allianz as an option for an additional cost. The cost is usually minimal, and it's based on the type of travel, destination, and length of your stay. I like Allianz Travel because they cover everything from medical and car rental insurance to covering lost or stolen items.

As my grandfather used to say, "It's better to have it and not need it, than to need it and not have it."

Pack A Universal Adapter

Everything runs on electricity. Our cell phones, sewing machines, irons, laptops, and even our ear buds. So it stands to reason that being able to charge these things while on the road is a must. Trust me, you don't want to see what I turn into when my cell phone battery dies. It's not pretty.

Most countries do not run on the same 110-120 volt electric grid we have here in the United States. Most use 220-240 voltage instead. Some countries even have odd-shaped electric plugs (like Ireland, those rebels). Therefore, depending on which country you're traveling to, you may need a travel adapter.

If you're not quite sure what all that means, that's ok. Just know that if you plug in your 110-volt US device into a 220-volt outlet in Europe without an adapter, it might explode. Or, at the very least, catch fire. No one wants that; am I right?

The universal adapters usually come in a cube-like device that you can plug directly into the wall in nearly any country and then you can safely plug in your American device into the adapter. I carry one on every international trip, whether I think I'll need it or not.

If you want to check for sure whether you need an adapter for your device, you can look for the "input" number either on the charger or the device itself. If you have one that says "INPUT: 100-240V," you're good to go. Just make sure to grab your magnifying glass first.

The good news is most cell phone charger blocks these days do have the 100-240V input number, which means they are travel adapters themselves. However, if you don't want to risk it (or you can't read writing that ridiculously small), you can find great universal travel adapters online.

Purchasing a universal adapter will cost anywhere from $15 to $40, depending on the manufacturer. You can find them either on Amazon or at your local AAA office.

Carry A Money Belt

If you're a fan of *Rick Steves' Europe* travel show as I am, I'm sure you've heard him mention a money belt a few times. But they actually are a good idea. Luckily the money belts of today are not like the fanny pack that thankfully fell out of style seemingly as quickly as it ventured in.

Many times, I've overheard horror stories in online travel groups of people storing their passport and other belongings in their hotel room safe only to have them stolen while they were out. If you think about it, the hotel staff also has access to your rooms and potentially those safes. So, as I tend to err on the side of paranoia, I refuse to leave any of my valuable belongings inside, especially my passport.

Therefore, I prefer to carry my passport with me at all times inside a money belt.

Money belts come in numerous styles and colors. I recommend finding one that can be worn comfortably around your waist, underneath your clothes. For me, I'm allergic to nickel. Therefore, I wear a money belt that has a plastic zipper and clasps.

Purchase A Prepaid Credit Card

When my son, Gavin, went on a student ambassador trip to Europe several years ago, we purchased a prepaid credit card for him to use while he was away. This way, he had a limited spending allowance and we could reload the card with more money if needed.

Because my son was only 16 years old at the time and couldn't even remember his glasses after he set them down, we hounded him over and over before he left: "Wallet, passport, and phone." Before he left his hotel room, before he got off the bus, before he got up from a restaurant, he needed to physically check to make sure he had his wallet, passport, and phone.

MY SON GAVIN

The good news is he actually did exactly what we said. No matter where he went, he always made sure his wallet, passport, and phone were on his person at all times. The bad news is this also stayed true as he walked into the Mediterranean Sea.

Yes, from that moment on, his wallet, passport, and phone were lost to the waters of the deep. Luckily, we the parents, as well as the student ambassador leaders all had copies of his passport. We were able to cancel the prepaid credit card, get the money back, and wire it to the ambassador leaders for my son to use on the remainder of his trip. Mom's plan wins again!

Even today, I like to carry a prepaid credit card on my international adventures just in case. If it gets lost or stolen, the card is not linked to any of my personal banking information, and the card can be canceled and the money returned.

To purchase a prepaid credit card, check with your local bank and/or AAA. There are usually fees involved as with any credit card, but these are minimal.

Add a Secured VPN to Your Devices

Data stealing is one of the most common crimes around the world today. Whenever you are logged in to public wi-fi, including at hotels, your devices are open to data thieves. For this reason, I have a secure Virtual Private Network (VPN) installed on my cell phone, tablet, and laptop.

A VPN is simply an application that you add to your mobile devices that protects you from data thieves. My husband could explain exactly how it works. As I am merely a civilian (and not a techie), I can just tell you it works. And it's very easy to install and use.

Many digital security networks offer a secure VPN. Personally, I prefer the Norton 360 VPN as I also use Norton security on all my devices. To add the VPN was only a few dollars more per month and it works across all of my devices.

Once the application is added to your cell phone or laptop, simply open the app and turn it on. Then, whenever you log in to a public wi-fi source (library, hotel, airport, coffee shop, etc.), the VPN application will do the rest.

Add An International Calling App On Your Phone

There are several reasons for using an international calling app on your cell phone. First, the cost savings. Unless you have an international calling account with your phone provider, the fees for making international calls are enormous. Some providers will allow you to add an international plan for one month, but again it usually comes with a hefty fee.

I still remember sitting in a Dublin coffee shop trying to log in to their wi-fi while texting my husband, trying to schedule a phone call. Even though I had added 1 month of international calling to my phone plan, the roaming fees and costs per minute were insanely high. So we played a continuous game of "Are you ready?" "Yes." "Are you sure?" "YES." "Ok, I'm turning on my roaming now, be ready!"

GRAFTON STREET, DUBLIN, IRELAND

Luckily, nowadays there are several apps you can add on your cell phone that are free to use and work internationally using your phone's data. The one my family uses the most is the "Signal" application. It is compatible with most cell phone services.

To avoid any extra data fees from your cell phone provider, I recommend limiting your calls to when you have access to wi-fi. Just don't forget to turn on your VPN first!

Call Your Bank Before You Leave

Have you ever been out of town and when you went to use your bank card, the card was declined? You know there's money in that account, but for some reason it just won't work. A little bit of panic sets in until you realize what happened: Not knowing you were out of town and thinking your card was stolen, your bank just shut off your card.

As I mentioned earlier, I recommend traveling with a prepaid credit card. However, if you prefer to use your bank card or personal credit card, be sure to contact your bank and/or credit card company to schedule your trip with them before you leave town. That way, when charges from a foreign country show up on your account, the automated systems won't mistakenly tag your card as stolen. Trust me, getting stuck in the middle of nowhere without access to any funds is a literal nightmare.

Keep All of Your Receipts

As Benjamin Franklin said in 1789, "... in this world nothing can be said to be certain, except death and taxes." This is especially true when traveling internationally.

Have you heard of a Value Added Tax (VAT)? If not, write it down. Commit it to memory. Because when you travel internationally, especially around Europe, you will be subject to VAT.

The VAT is a tax that many countries add to all goods and services. The total amount of VAT can vary by country and usually ranges between 17 - 27%. The average is around 21%. That is on top of any other fees that may apply to your purchase. It really puts our average sales tax of 7.25% here in the United States into perspective, right?

The good news is that as a foreign passport holder, you can most likely get the VAT payments refunded to you. However, to do so there are few things you must remember.

When making a purchase, present your passport to the cashier and ask them for a tax-free form. This will then be attached to the receipt you receive after making your purchase.

Keep ALL of your receipts. This includes hotel stays, shopping, food purchases, etc. I like to carry an envelope with me to collect them all as I travel.

Before you leave the country in which you made the purchase(s), you'll need to present your receipts and fill out VAT forms to request your refund. This can be done at the customs office, usually located inside the airport or train station. Be prepared to stand in line.

✈ **PRO TIP:** *To avoid currency exchange rates, opt to have the funds sent to your credit card.*

One thing to also keep in mind is most countries have a minimum total purchase in order for you to get the VAT refunded. For instance, in Iceland you must spend a minimum of approximately $41 US dollars for the purchase to be eligible for a VAT refund.

To view the current VAT rates, visit Taxfoundation.org.

To view current currency exchange rates, visit x-rates.com.

Duty-Free Shops

When I first heard of the duty-free shops I thought, "Oh my gosh, purchases without paying taxes, yes please!" Unfortunately, the reality was not exactly that simple.

A duty-free shop is a store located inside most airports where you can make purchases without paying a "duty" or a tax. However, because of the various costs of running the shop, you'll probably find most of the same items cheaper on Amazon.

The main exceptions to this rule are items that tend to have a bigger customs import fee like tobacco, alcohol, fragrances, and cosmetics. Honestly, I can't really speak to the tobacco, fragrance, or cosmetics as I don't really use those products. The alcohol one, on the other hand, I can sort of attest to.

My husband is a whiskey snob so much so, he loves to collect them and pair them with different cigars. It's his thing. So, when I went to Ireland, I wanted to find him a special whiskey for his cabinet. Unfortunately, after I had already bought a special bottle of Greenspot for him, he sent me a message asking me to find him another brand. Oh, boy.

WHISKEY BAR IN DUBLIN

Luckily, I found the bottle he was requesting. What wasn't so lucky is I then had to get two full bottles of whiskey back to the United States. While in the liquor store, I asked the owner for her suggestion. She told me that she goes back and forth to the States at least twice a year for conventions and such. She told me to just put the bottles in my suitcase, check my bag with the airline, and forget about them. So that's what I did.

After throwing away an old pair of sneakers to make room in my suitcase, I carefully packed the bottles between several layers of clothes for protection and the bag made it home with no issues. However, when I looked inside the duty-free shop at the bottles for sale, they were significantly cheaper than what I had just paid (by the way, there are no VAT returns for alcohol).

In any case, I can't really recommend or not recommend shopping at a Duty-Free shop. However, before you make a purchase, I do recommend checking Amazon to compare prices.

COTTON QUILT IN GRANITE FALLS, NORTH CAROLINA

CHAPTER TWO

Quilt Shop Hop Road Trips

WHAT IS A SHOP HOP?

Quite simply, a shop hop is when quilters hit the road to visit multiple quilt shops in a single trip, or over the course of a few days. Some are organized shop hops, where a group of specific quilt shops join together and create some sort of passport system to encourage quilters to visit their shops.

There are many levels of organized quilt shop hops, including those put on by just a small group of quilt shops to larger ones that are run state-wide. There are even a handful of organized shop hops that are nationwide.

Usually, each participating quilt shop will offer some sort of incentive, or a "thank you" for visiting their shop. This can be anything from a free block pattern (or whole quilt pattern) to a free fat quarter. Others will offer grand prize drawings for those who visit all of the participating shops. I've seen some pretty great gift baskets given away, chock full of fabric, notions, and other goodies. One organized shop hop even gave away a sewing machine!

TRUTH

One of the great things about shop hops is that each quilt shop has something unique to offer. Some quilt shops specialize in batiks, while some focus on a particular brand, like Moda or Free Spirit. Some have thousands of quilt patterns, while others have rooms filled with notions and gadgets. There's sure to be something for everyone.

But the main reason for going on a shop hop is the fun! Not only do you get out and see new places, but you may even find quilt shops you didn't know existed.

For instance, on my first big shop hop road trip we found one of my favorite little quilts shop called The Cotton Quilt in Granite Falls, NC. Hidden away in the middle of farmland is a little white house that has been turned into a quilt shop! The entire house is the quilt shop, and every room has a different theme, including the kitchen!

Here in North Carolina, we are lucky to have several organized shop hops. In fact, the *Quilt! Carolina Shop Hop* has become an annual event for me. It started a few years ago when I took a handful of my students along for a weekend trip to visit 8 of the 12 participating quilt shops.

It was an absolute blast! Between sharing stories in the car, seeing new places, meeting new friends around the state, petting all the lovely fabric, and somehow getting lost while still following the GPS, we all walked away with great memories!

HOW TO PLAN A SHOP HOP

A couple of years ago, I took one of those personality tests that show which of the main 7 trait categories you fall under. Me? I fell under 2 categories equally. The People Pleaser and the Planner. Which mostly means I love to plan things and I really, really hope everyone loves what I planned.

Looking back, I've basically been a project planner for most of my life. Even when I was a kid, I enjoyed planning my school projects much more than actually accomplishing them. In fact, it was almost as if once the plan was in place, my work was done. Or so it seemed to me, anyway.

Over the years, I've planned four state-to-state moves (including our 3,000-

CRAZY HORSE MONUMENT IN SOUTH DAKOTA

ON THE ROAD TO DEVILS TOWER

DEVILS TOWER, WYOMING

mile trek from Washington State to North Carolina) and more "just for fun" road trips than I can even remember. So, you might say that when it comes to planning shop hop road trips, I'm your girl.

To best illustrate my planning process, I'll continue by using the example of the North Carolina mountains trip along the Blue Ridge Parkway described in the earlier Budgeting chapter.

Where Am I Going?

After doing a little research on the quilt shops located along the Blue Ridge parkway in the North Carolina mountains, I found a fairly large mountain town called Boone. There are two quilt shops located in Boone and plenty of options for lodging, so it seemed like the perfect place to begin my trip. From there, I decided I would work my way west along the Blue Ridge Parkway toward Asheville, NC.

Now, if you haven't been to the Blue Ridge Parkway, I highly suggest you add it to your bucket list. Known as "America's Favorite Drive," the Blue Ridge Parkway stretches 469 miles from Cherokee, North Carolina, all the way to Afton, Virginia.

Along the parkway, you'll find some of the oldest mountains in the world, the deepest gorge east of the Grand Canyon, breath taking views, arts and crafting facilities, barn quilt trails, and at least two dozen quilt shops along the entire

BLUE RIDGE PARKWAY, NORTH CAROLINA

route. As I said, the Blue Ridge Parkway is a must-do road trip.

However, for this particular trip I only had a few days to work with, and as you can imagine, 469 miles will take more than a few days. So, Boone to Asheville would have to do.

How Long Will I Be On The Road?

If you don't already have a set time limit, to figure out how long your trip will be, the first thing you need to know is how many quilt shops you plan to visit. For most shop hop road trips, you can realistically plan to visit 2 to 3 quilt shops per day, depending on how far apart they are. Also, you can plan to spend an average of 1 hour in each quilt shop.

Now, I am fully aware that I can spend several hours in a single quilt shop. Especially when I get to talking with the staff and other customers about a project. However, after taking several shop hop road trips throughout the years, I did the math. Even with our shop hop groups of 4 – 6 people, we still only averaged about 1 hour in each quilt shop.

For my Blue Ridge Parkway shop hop road trip, I planned to visit a total of 5 quilt shops. Therefore, I knew I would need at least 2 – 3 days minimum to visit them all.

When I plan a multi-day road trip, I like to use an online guide to help me see everything laid out. There are several websites you can use for this, and they each have their pros and cons.

For instance, GoogleMaps.com is most people's "go to" website. However, you will need to know your route ahead of time as Google Maps does not give those suggestions. It does, however, give you driving time between locations, including toll roads and traffic jams. And Google Maps also gives suggestions for dining and where to stay, which is helpful.

If you don't know your route ahead of time, I like to use a website called Furkot.com. With Furkot.com, you can add your destination points-including all of the quilt shops-and Furkot.com will plan the best driving route for you. It will tell you where to start and the easiest routes in between. Furkot.com will also give you suggestions on where to stay and other fun things to do in the area you'll be visiting.

Both Google Maps and Furkot.com are free to use.

If you have an RV for longer routes, or plan to do a lot of road tripping, you can also use Roadtrippers.com. This is one of the best online websites for planning road trips. Roadtrippers has everything from live maps (with traffic advisories) to hotel and food suggestions and more. There is also a section with tips and suggestions from other travelers. However, to get the full benefit, there

ALABAMA HILLS, CALIFORNIA

ROAD TRIP ITINERARY

DAY 1	
Drive to Boone, NC	5 hrs

DAY 2	
Breakfast at homestay	1 hr
Drive to first quilt shop	30 min
Time at first quilt shop	1 hr
Drive to second quilt shop	30 min
Time at second quilt shop	1 hr
Lunch	1½ hrs
Sight-seeing	3 hrs
Dinner	1½ hrs

DAY 3	
Breakfast at homestay	1 hr
Drive to third quilt shop	1 hr
Time at third quilt shop	1 hr
Drive to fourth quilt shop	30 min
Time at third quilt shop	1 hr
Lunch	1½ hrs
Sight-seeing	3 hrs
Dinner	1½ hrs

DAY 4	
Breakfast at homestay	1 hr
Drive to fifth quilt shop	1 hr
Time at fifth quilt shop	1 hr
Sight-seeing	1 hr
Lunch	1½ hrs
Sight-seeing	3 hrs
Dinner	1½ hrs

DAY 5	
Drive Home	5 hrs

is a yearly fee.

The next thing you want to add to your shop hop road trip plan is food. I usually like to plan at least 1 hour per meal if I've packed a lunch. Or I will plan 1 ½ hours if I plan to eat out. That extra half hour allows extra time for driving to and from your lunch destination.

Next, I like to add in plenty of extra time to "see the sights." On this particular shop hop road trip to the Blue Ridge Parkway, I added in 3 hours each day of extra time. And oh my gosh, was I glad I did! More on that later.

So far, I knew I needed at least 5 hours to visit 5 quilt shops and 3 hours each day for extra sight-seeing. Adding in lunches and dinners I knew I would need 3 full days of visiting and an extra 2 days of travel to and from my house. Therefore, my total shop hop road trip would require 5 days.

With my plan to find a homestay lodging somewhere in the middle of all the quilt shop locations, and using Furkot.com to track my drive times, here's what my itinerary looked like.

Obviously, there will be some give and take when you're actually out on the road. But as

ANTIQUE'S MAIN, BLOWING ROCK, NORTH CAROLINA

long as you give yourself wiggle room, you should have plenty of time to see and do all the things on your list. Plus, you never know when you might run into a great antique mall and find your first Singer machine!

If I haven't mentioned it before, I love antique stores. Stopping at antique stores is almost as much fun on shop hops as the actual quilt shops! So when I was driving along near the Blue Ridge Parkway and happened to round a corner and see a gigantic sign that said, "Antique Mall", you know I had to stop.

And boy, what an antique store. This place was HUGE! It was a warehouse that had been turned into two stories of shopping. Hanging from all the balconies were gorgeous handmade quilts. Rummaging through the many

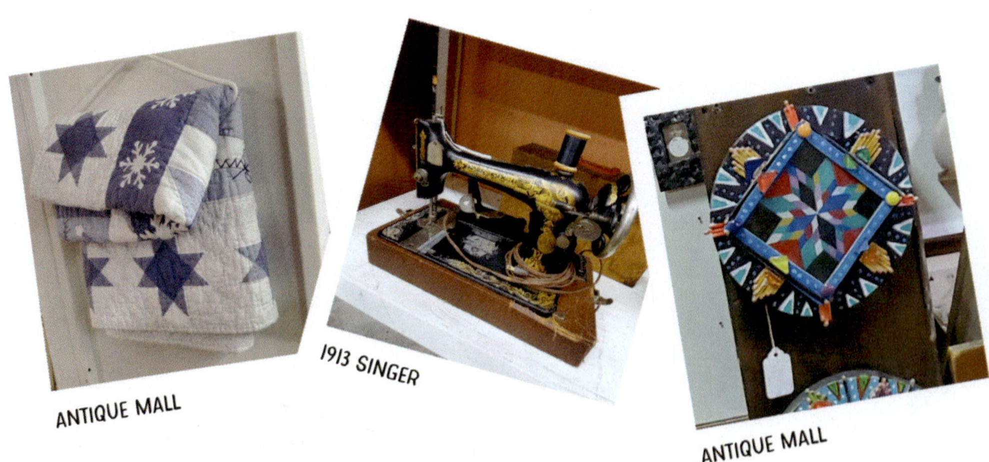

ANTIQUE MALL

1913 SINGER

ANTIQUE MALL

stacks, I found probably 50 more quilts of all different sizes, fabrics, and techniques. I had entirely too much fun spreading them out and admiring the work that went into each one.

Sadly, none of the quilts came home with me. However, as I was making my way along the far wall, I happened to look down. On the bottom shelf, half hidden, was a Singer machine. Of course, I jumped down to pull it out of its cubby spot, and sure enough: This was a gorgeous old Singer sewing machine, complete with case cover.

The price tag said $50 and "it works" so I snatched it up quicker than you can shake a stick, and off to the checkout I went. Surprisingly, the owner didn't even know she had the machine on the shelf. All the better for me, as I've been eyeing these machines for a long time. But this was the first I found one in the wild.

After getting home and looking up the serial number on the Singer website, I discovered that this machine was born in 1913 and predates the Featherweight machines by 20 years!

Take it from me, you never know what you're going to find on your next shop hop road trip!

WHAT TO PACK

I have been taking road trips for most of my life. Even as a child I looked forward to hitting the road with my mother in her old '77 Caprice Classic. That car was only a year older than me, and we took it all over the West Coast. I remember trips from Washington State to Bandon, Oregon, for family reunions and beach trips to Seaside, Oregon, to watch the sea lions. We even drove all the way to San Diego, California, to see family in Escondido and visit Disneyland. That was back when they had the original *Pirates of the Caribbean* ride (pre-Johnny Depp era) and you had to wait in line 2 hours minimum to ride the Matterhorn. No express passes or e-tickets for us!

DISNEYLAND

However, all those road trips over the years helped teach me what items are absolutely necessary for a successful road trip and which you can leave at home.

When packing for a road trip, there are 4 lists you need to make: Just in Case Items, Lunch Stop Items, In the Cooler Items, and Everything Else.

Just In Case Items

Generally speaking, all of your "just in case" items will go in the trunk. These include the items you should only need to pull out in an emergency.

1. EMERGENCY KIT

No matter if you're headed to a neighboring town or out of state, it always a good idea to carry an emergency kit in the trunk. Just make sure to keep an eye on the expiration dates for some of the items inside. There's nothing worse than getting out the flashlight only to find the batteries have expired.

2. EXTRA QUILT

Yes, I always carry an extra quilt in my trunk. No, not just the ones I'm working on. There are several reasons I carry a finished quilt in the trunk: in case the car breaks down or I have to pull over for a nap somewhere, or even something simple like bundling up to go see a movie. I'm the type of person that is always cold. My son jokingly refers to me as "ice queen" because I'm seemingly always that cold. Honestly, they could raise the air conditioning temperature above zero degrees once in a while.

3. RE-USABLE TOTE BAGS

Where are my fellow bag addicts at? Over the years I have tried several different patterns for re-usable tote bags. However, I could never find one that was sturdy enough to handle the amount of weight I tend to stuff in them. Finally, I decided to create my own re-usable tote bag pattern.

Truthfully, I use re-usable tote bags for EVERYTHING. From grocery shopping to quilt shop hops to sewing with my girls. Even on longer road trips, this bag will come in handy. You can fit so much stuff in them, including those great 12 x 12 plastic project boxes!

Be sure to check the Quilt Projects chapter toward the end of this book for the full re-usable tote bag pattern.

4. LAUNDRY BASKET

I learned this next little tip from my mom. You know how most of us just throw things in the trunk and hope they don't roll around and fall out of bags? Well, Mom's solution is she always keeps a laundry basket in the trunk. On road trips, this comes in especially handy because you can keep all of your smaller items in one place rather than digging through the trunk, thinking "I KNOW I have my bathroom bag in here somewhere!"

My favorite basket to keep in my trunk is collapsible. It's sturdy enough to

APPALACHIAN MOUNTAINS

hold most items and can collapse down to save space if needed. You can find a few different collapsible laundry baskets on Amazon.com. They cost about $25 - $30 each.

WEST VIRGINIA WELCOME CENTER

Lunch Stop Items

Remember that re-usable tote bag I mentioned? Get one out. We're going to load it up. Heck, get out two. Here's what we're going to put in them.

1. RE-USABLES

In order to save money, I like to pack my own food for my road trips. This means sandwich stuff, snacks, etc. Rest stops and State Welcome Centers are great places to stop for a quick lunch on the road. Just make sure you've come prepared.

We used to bring paper plates and bowls with us on all our road trips. We even had those wicker plate-holders so our paper plates didn't fall apart. However, in the last few years I've found that using re-usable bowls, plates, and plastic-ware is much easier and takes up less room. Not to mention they are much better for the environment.

2. CLEAN UP SUPPLIES

The next item I suggest adding to your re-usable tote bags is one or two empty garbage bags, a dish towel or two, a handful of Ziploc bags, and a roll of paper towels. You would be amazed how often those paper towels come in handy. For instance, during my last visit to the Mancuso Quilt Show in Virginia, I took a fabulous fabric dying class with my friend Cindy Lohbeck. Between myself and the other ladies in class, we used the entire roll!

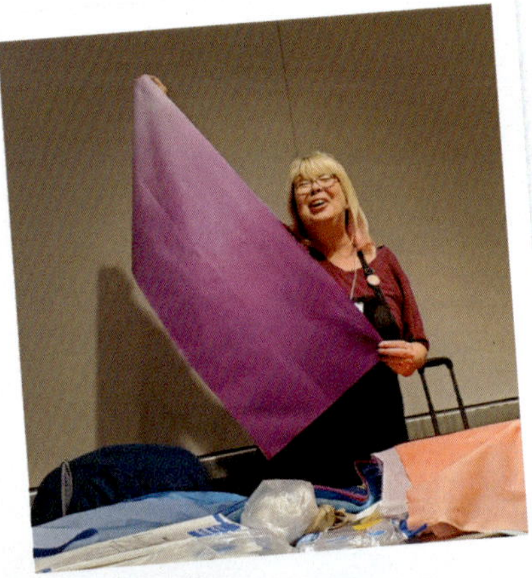

CINDY LOHBECK

Also, in a pinch, a garbage bag can be used for collecting dirty laundry or wet clothes from an impromptu afternoon at the beach. And the large Ziploc bags are great for storing dirty dishes until you get to your hotel to wash them.

In The Cooler Items

Taking a cooler with me on a road trip is an absolute must – not just because I eat meals on the road and can carry all my snacks, but also because I like my water bottles to stay cold.

GAVIN AND THE FREMONT TROLL IN SEATTLE

1. THE COOLER

The type of vehicle you are driving and how many items you want to carry will dictate the size of travel cooler you'll need. For my road trips I usually carry water bottles, sliced fruit and veggies, and occasionally a small bottle of milk inside. Therefore, I take a smaller 12-can size expandable soft-sided cooler. It fits perfectly just behind the center console so anyone in the car can reach into it on the road.

TRAVELING QUILTER TRAVEL MUG

2. WATER BOTTLES

I drink a LOT of water. However, on road trips I hate going through so many plastic bottles. Plus, they take up so much room! Mom's solution to that problem is to freeze 2 – 3 bottles of water the night before you leave. Then, place them in the bottom of your cooler the next morning.

This solves 2 problems. First, the frozen bottles replace those freezer packs, which saves room. Second, you can drink the water as they melt. And once you get to your hotel or homestay lodging, you can refill them and stick them back in the freezer to use again the next day. Win/win!

Along with the frozen water bottles, I also keep my trusty Traveling Quilter travel mug with me. It keeps your hot drinks hot and your cold drinks cold!

Everything Else

There are just a few more items that I suggest adding to your ultimate road trip shop hop packing list.

1. LITTLE PURSE KIT

Many years ago, we were touring the Kings Mountain Battlefield in North Carolina with my cousin and her family when her son fell and scraped his knee. I quickly pulled out my trusty little purse kit and got him patched up in no time. My cousin laughed and accused me of being "that mom." Even though my son now has a family of his own I still wear that badge proudly. And I still carry my trusty little purse kit everywhere I go.

Here is a list of everything I carry inside my little purse kit:

- Band-Aids®
- Neosporin
- Antiseptic wipes
- Small sewing kit
- Ibuprofen (or aspirin)
- Small notebook and pen
- Clothes-pins
- Paper clips
- Safety pins
- Hand sanitizer
- Touchless opener

2. SINK CLEANING SUPPLIES

Because I travel with my re-usable plastic ware, bowls, and plates, I need to keep them clean. So in my travel case I also carry a collapsible cleaning basin that can be used even with a hotel room sink. Simply pop it open, fill it with soap and water, and you're ready to go. As it's collapsible, it takes up little space. Plus, it can be used to wash clothes as well.

Similar to the reusable collapsible laundry basket, you can find the smaller dish cleaning basin on Amazon.com for around $15 - $20.

3. OVERNIGHT BAG

I am a night driver. Mostly because I make so many unplanned stops along my route ("Oh look, a history marker sign. Let's stop!"), I tend to arrive at many destinations after dark. Therefore, I like to keep an overnight bag packed and inside the car with me. Inside the overnight bag I pack my bathroom supplies, any medications, pajamas, and one change of clothes.

This way, when I arrive at my destination, I can just grab my purse and overnight bag and go in without even opening the trunk. It's a safety thing as well as a convenience. You can always grab the rest of your stuff from the trunk in the morning when there's daylight.

HOW TO ORGANIZE YOUR TRUNK

Let's face it: Organizing your trunk space can be a bit like playing a game of Tetris. There's only so much room to put so much stuff. Also, the more people in the car, the more "suggestions" available for how to fit everything into such a small space. However, to help out I've devised a way to fit everything you need into one small space - the trunk.

Rather than trying to force everything to fit, you can strategically place items in the trunk so you have easier access to the things you may need along the road.

Step One: Place the big items first. This includes your large suitcase(s) that you won't need to get into until you've reached your final destination. Try to get them to the very back.

The next items to go in the trunk are the ones you will most likely need to have readily available. This includes your laundry basket full of things like your emergency kit, lunch stop items, etc.

Finally, everything else can go in between. Especially any extra pillows and/or quilts you are traveling with can be squished into smaller spaces in between other larger items.

But my biggest tip of all is LEAVE EXTRA ROOM FOR FABRIC!

PACKED FOR A ROAD TRIP

THREAD OF SUCCESS

This tip may seem like common sense. However, you'd be surprised how often I've forgotten to plan ahead for everything I may bring home.

In 2019, I attended my first Fall Quilt Market in Houston, Texas. I took part in their brand-new program "Threads of Success." It was a program specifically for new businesses in the quilting industry.

The program was everything I could have imagined and more. We got to attend lectures from some of the top quilting industry professionals and ask questions. We got to explore the Quilt Market floor as well as be mentored by a handful of industry professionals. Unfortunately, I did not make it into Tula Pink's group, but there's always hope for a future Quilt Market!

As the show progressed, between our "welcome bags" and all of the samples I garnered, I began to realize that all of my goodies were never going to fit inside my suitcase. I'd had no idea I'd be getting anything on this adventure, let alone enough stuff to fill up its own suitcase. So on the last day of Market, there I was calling an rideshare to take me to the nearest Target (across town) to buy

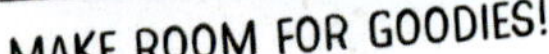

MAKE ROOM FOR GOODIES!

QUILT MARKET LOOT

an extra suitcase. It was only after making it home I discovered the convention center has a mailing service. Oh well, live and learn.

After that ordeal, making room for all my purchases is now the first thing I think of when I begin to load the car.

Of course, there's no way to know exactly how much room you'll need or what you are going to buy on the road. But one thing you can be sure of is that you WILL be bringing home more than you left with. So it's a good idea to make sure your trunk is not too overloaded at the beginning of your trek.

Another idea is to have each person leave some extra space in their suitcases. That way there's less extra trunk space required for the ride home.

With a little preparation and a great packing list, you'll have everything you need for a fabulous shop hop road trip!

CHARLOTTE TENNESSEE 470 MILES
CHARLOTTE MAINE 1164 MILES
CHARLOTTE TEXAS 1275 MILES
CHARLOTTE VERMONT 893 MILES
CHARLOTTE IOWA 940 MILES
CHARLOTTE WATERS, AUSTRALIA 9,975 MILES
CHARLOTTE HALL, MARYLAND 390 MILES
CHARLOTTE NORTH CAROLINA
THE CENTER OF THE KNOWN WORLD!

CAROLINA LILY QUILT SHOW

CHAPTER THREE

Quilt Show Adventures

WHY GO TO A QUILT SHOW?

The very first quilt show I ever attended was the Carolina Lily quilt show here in North Carolina. It is a guild quilt show that is put on annually by our local Charlotte Quilters Guild. Little did I know that years later I'd not only be a guild member but also volunteering for the board.

At its core, a quilt show is a place where quilters gather together to put a bunch of quilts on display for all to enjoy. However, over the years many quilt shows have grown to include workshops and demonstrations as well as a vendor mall. The vendor mall is where you'll find everything from quilting gadgets, notions, books, fabric, and even sewing machines and quilting tables for sale from businesses all over the quilting industry.

OSQE RALEIGH QUILT SHOW

Going into that first quilt show, I had no idea what to expect. And to be honest, I was a little overwhelmed. However, because the Carolina Lily quilt show is a smaller-size show I was able to see and experience pretty much everything in one day. I had a blast! I mean, new quilting friends, quilting gadgets, new fabrics, workshops, and amazing quilts all in one place? What's not to love?

When I decided to try my hand at my first national-size quilt show in Raleigh, North Carolina, I was out of my league. Because I didn't know to plan ahead, I missed out on all the classes I wanted to take, didn't have enough time to visit all the vendor booths, and even missed several of the free demonstrations. I was utterly disappointed.

But I didn't let that stop me. Instead of being discouraged, I decided to do a little research and use my experience in Raleigh as a lesson so that I'd be better prepared for the next big quilt show.

And I'm so glad I did! Since that first Carolina Lily quilt show, I've now been a vendor at that very same quilt show and attended dozens more quilt shows of all shapes and sizes - everything from local quilt guild shows to national, international, and even the Quilt Market Trade Show in Houston, Texas. Unfortunately, Quilt Market is only for businesses in the Quilting industry. However, it is immediately followed by the Fall International Quilt Festival, which most of the vendors, teachers, and designers stay to attend as well. You never know who you'll run into!

To be prepared for your first (or next) big quilt show, let's first go over the different types of quilt shows available.

CAROLINA LILY QUILT SHOW

Guild Show

Quilt guilds are basically a group of quilters who get together each month to share their quilts, learn new techniques, and discuss all things quilting related. They're very much a fellowship of quilters. In fact,

MY BOOTH AT CAROLINA LILY QUILT SHOW

OSQE RALIEGH QUILT SHOW

these quilt guilds have become so popular, you can probably find one near where you live, if you haven't joined one already.

Many of the larger-size quilt guilds require membership dues to join and use those funds to bring in guest teachers each month for the members to learn everything from techniques to the latest quilting gadgets and everything in between. And to bring in even more funds for even bigger-name quilting teachers, many quilt guilds will host an annual or biennial quilt show.

These guild quilt shows are usually of smaller size and it's easy to experience them completely in a single day. You can usually expect to see quilts by the guild members on display and quilts made by others in the community, as well as a few local vendors. Many times, the local quilt shops will have a booth set up as well!

Quilting Marketplace

Some may argue that a quilting marketplace is not technically a quilt show. I suppose that depends on how you define "quilt show." For instance, if you are looking mainly for finished quilts on display, workshops, and/or demonstrations, then the quilting marketplace may not be right for you.

The quilting marketplace is a "show" that brings together several quilting vendors so you can conveniently shop with them all in one place. In fact, a true quilting marketplace is somewhat of a rarity. Currently, I only know of one that is put on here in North Carolina each January, but I'm sure there are more around the country I have yet to find.

National Quilt Show

The most common of quilt shows visited each year are the national quilt shows. These quilt shows are larger than a guild quilt show and are usually organized by a large group and/or business. In contrast to a guild quilt show, the national shows will have a much larger selection of quilts on display for you to enjoy as well as an offering of quilting classes throughout the show's duration.

Each national quilt show generally lasts 3 - 4 days and, depending on how many classes you attend, may take at least 2 days to visit in their entirety. Their

AUTHOR AND DESIGNER KIMBERLY EINMO

QUILT ARTIST BEVERLY Y. SMITH

AUTHOR AND DESIGNER CHRISTA WATSON

QUILTER AND INSTRUCTOR CINDY LOHBECK

AUTHORS AND DESIGNERS KAFFE FASSET AND BRANDON MABLY

QUILTER AND MUSICIAN RICKY TIMS

vendor malls welcome many different vendors from all over the country (some international vendors as well), who offer everything from unique fabrics to gadgets, sewing machines, and even quilting tables.

Also, many national quilt shows will present short 15 - or 30 - minute free demos throughout each day that give the vendors an opportunity to show you how to use their particular products and answer questions you may have.

QuiltCon

Every year in February, the international Modern Quilt Guild puts on the largest modern quilt show of its kind. Taking place in a different location around the United States each year, QuiltCon focuses on the art of modern quilting. They include over 600 quilts on display with at least 2/3 of them juried in from the Modern Quilt Guild members around the world.

In addition to the quilts, QuiltCon also hosts a number of quilting discussion panels, a full vendor mall, and workshops for every skill level featuring top designers and teachers.

For more information on their upcoming show, visit www.quiltcon.com.

International Quilt Show

An international quilt show is the granddaddy of all quilt shows. These shows bring together quilters, teachers, and vendors from all over the world to one location for several days of quilting magic.

You can expect to spend at least 3 - 5 days at an international quilt show. But even then, you probably won't be able to see and experience everything, between multiple classes happening each day, hundreds of vendors, and an incredible array of amazing quilts on display presented by some of the top quilters in the world. You can also expect to find some of the top quilting teachers from around the world offering classes on their newest and greatest techniques and more.

One of the best things about international quilt shows is that not only do you get to see the incredible quilting talent, but you also get to experience firsthand the cultures in which these artists reside. Each country's quilters have their own unique style and viewpoints that they bring to their quilts.

Currently there are seven main international quilt shows held each year.

- Birmingham Festival of Quilts in Birmingham, England, UK
- Fall International Quilt Festival in Houston, TX, USA
- Spring International Quilt Festival held in a new location each spring in the USA
- Tokyo Quilt Festival in Tokyo, Japan

ORIGINAL SEWING
& QUILT EXPO,
RALIEGH, NC

JANOME

- Patchwork Sitges in Barcelona, Spain
- Australian Quilt Convention in Melbourne, Australia
- Carrefour Europeen du Patchwork in Val d'Argent, France

In 2017, Nancy Zieman took a poll of her fans and asked them, "What is your focus when attending a sewing or quilting show?" Overwhelmingly, people spoke about how much inspiration and knowledge they get from quilt shows. From the classes, demonstrations, and just chatting up your fellow quilters, you can learn more than you ever imagined at quilt shows.

However, my favorite quote came from a lady named Londa in Northwood, Ohio. Londa said, "In every quilt show, there is creativity abounding. We just need that spark to take on the next masterpiece!" I couldn't have said it better myself.

KNOW BEFORE YOU GO

As I discovered the hard way at my first national quilt show, it's always a good idea to plan ahead when visiting quilt shows. Some of the larger ones especially can be overwhelming. However, with a little pre-planning and knowing where to look, you'll be sure to make the best of every quilt show travel adventure.

Pre-Register For The Quilt Show

Registering online prior to the quilt show can be beneficial for two reasons. First, some of the quilt shows will offer special events or trinkets for people who pre-register ahead of time. For instance, at the Mid-Atlantic Quilt Festival in Virginia Beach one year, we were given the opportunity to get access to the vendor mall the day BEFORE the quilt show opened.

FABRICAHOLIC!

I particularly appreciated the opportunity to walk the floor to see what all the vendors had to offer before the mad rush of quilt show visitors arrived the next day. Plus, it allowed me more time during the quilt show to take a few classes.

Second, many of the classes will sell out. Most quilt shows will announce their list of workshops on their website months in advance. In fact, many of them also have a newsletter where they will let you

FROND FABRICS AT OSQE ATLANTA

JAN MARIE LARSON OF THIMBLES FOR YOU

know via email the moment new classes are posted. If there is one you know you want to take, sign up as soon as possible. The last thing you want is to show up at the quilt show and find that all your favorite classes are sold out.

You can also follow many quilt shows (and/or quilting guilds) on social media. This is another great way to find out show information and class announcements.

Preview the Vendor Mall

This one is pretty important and it's one I learned the hard way. At the national and international quilt show level, I've seen as many as 200 vendors. Crazy, right? You need an actual map to figure out where each of them is located.

So what I started doing is checking the quilt show website well in advance of the show date and printing out their list of vendors. Then, I go through the list and circle which ones I know I'll want to visit. This could depend on which vendors I'm familiar with or what items I need for a new project.

I wasn't kidding about the map. Many of the larger shows will provide a vendor mall map when you check in on the first day of the quilt show. So, while drinking your coffee, have a sit, go through the map and highlight each of your priority vendors; then plan your walking route. This way you're much less likely to miss one.

Of course, the vendor mall is always filled with fabulous goodies that you didn't expect, so be sure to plan extra time for walking the floor. You know, for those moments when that pretty fabric calls out to you across the aisle.

Look for the Demos

One of my favorite things at a large quilt show is the demonstrations. Many of the vendors are given 15 - 30 minutes to wow you with their best products and techniques. These can give you a fantastic amount of inspiration for your own projects as well as let you see how the gadgets are best used. It's kind of like those demo booths at giant fairs but better. Some may even provide you with a coupon!

> ✈ **PRO TIP:** *When you first arrive at the quilt show and are given your "welcome packet," be sure to take a few extra minutes to go over the list of demonstrations and set alarms on your cell phone to remind you when they're about to start. Losing track of time at a quilt show is unavoidable. I can't tell you how many demonstrations I've missed due to getting caught up at a vendor booth or just chatting with a new quilting friend.*

Set Your Budget

Let's be honest, we can all go a little crazy at quilt shows. I'm certainly no exception. Heck, I have a problem keeping to my budget at local quilt shops, let alone an international quilt show. However, sitting at home with your bank balance in hand, you can make a more measured plan for how much you can truly afford to spend at the quilt show.

For a detailed refresher on budgeting your quilting travel adventure, flip back to the "Budgeting Your Quilting Adventure" section at the beginning of this book.

Take Time to Explore the Show

Every quilt show is a little different, which is part of why they're so much fun to visit. However, generally they all offer 3 main things: shopping, workshops, and quilts. Therefore, you want to make sure you have time to experience as

OSQE ATLANTA

much of each as you can.

Most quilt shows last on average 2 or 3 days, depending on their size. I've found the best way to experience quilt shows (and do a little exploring) is to break them down by day and event.

KAFFE FASSETT QUILT CLASS

When you first arrive at the quilt show, you'll want to pick up your registration packet whether you pre-registered online or not. This will usually include a welcome brochure listing all the activities going on at the quilt show and may even include a few vendor coupons. Who doesn't love a good coupon?

CLASS DAY

I usually like to sign up for at least one class at each show. This way I get to learn a little something new and meet the teachers. Yes, you can learn many things online, but nothing beats the in-person tidbits and little extras you get from attending the quilt show classes.

OFF THE WALL QUILT

I reserve this day for classes only, so I rarely even step foot on the main floor. Plus, if I only sign up for a half-day class, it leaves more time for me to visit a local museum or art gallery around the city.

QUILT FLOOR DAY

This is the big day. Depending on the size of the quilt show, you'll want to plan about 3 hours visiting the vendors and about 2 hours for viewing the quilts. Obviously, these times will vary from show to show, but it's a good estimate. Plus, don't forget about those demo times!

> ✈ **PRO TIP:** *Scout out the bathrooms as soon as you arrive. As corny as this may sound, there's nothing worse than being in the middle of the vendor mall and that little tingle hits you but you have no idea where the nearest restroom is located. Yes, I speak from experience on this one. Ever since then, I've made it a point to always know where the bathrooms are the moment I arrive.*

MORE THAN JUST A QUILT SHOW

Attending a great quilt show can be an adventure in itself. However, what if you have some extra time between classes or after the show has closed for the day? That is when your trip becomes a truly grand adventure.

Not too many years ago, packing the entire family into the back of a station wagon and hitting the open road to see the "world's biggest ball of string" or the "biggest frying pan" was actually the norm. The classic *National Lampoon's Vacation* movie comes to mind. Somehow, those long road trips became a thing of the past.

Well, I say we bring them back!

Each year (when not in a pandemic), I travel to at least a dozen or so quilt shows and/or shop hops around the United States. Because I'm also a museum lover and history buff, I like to explore the cities I visit to see what I can find.

In 2019, I made my annual trek to Reno, Nevada, for my mother's birthday. On this particular visit, my parents had recently purchased a small motor home. So we decided to take it on its maiden voyage. Off to California we went.

Over the 10 years or so I lived in Nevada, I'd made the trek between Reno and Big Pine, California, many times. We had extended family that lived in that area. FYI: If you're ever in nearby Bishop, California, be sure to stop by Erick Schat's Bakery. You won't be disappointed!

Until this particular road trip, Big Pine was the farthest south I'd traveled. So this time we decided to drive a little further down the road. About 20 miles south of Lone Pine, California, we found the Manzanar Historical Site. Located in the middle of the open desert, this site was the home of the Manzanar War Relocation Center during WWII. Many of the Japanese Americans housed there were brought from Bainbridge Island in Washington State; where part of my family lives today.

SCHATS BAKERY BIG PINE CA

Inside the museum hangs an incredible handmade wall hanging quilt made by Hannah Takagi Homes. Having lived at Manzanar with her family when she was young, Hannah presented the quilt in 1988 as an honor to all those once housed there. This beautiful quilt looks

MANZANAR CAMP

WORLD LARGEST CHEST OF DRAWERS

to be made of wool, cotton, and string.

One of my favorite things about taking road trips is getting to see all of these amazing little treasures the United States has to offer. Did you know that here in North Carolina we have the biggest dresser? Seriously! There's even giant socks hanging out of one of the drawers. It drives the OCD in me crazy.

But how do you go about finding all these great places to visit? Well, start by asking uncle Google.

The first thing I do when researching a planned road trip is to do an online search. I go to Google.com and type in "things to do in Nevada" (or wherever your destination may be). Google will provide a list of results, such as "Top 15 Must See Places in Nevada." I then do a quick scan and click on a couple of the links that sound interesting. From there it's just a matter of scrolling through the lists and picking a few that sound like fun.

Of course, if you're looking for the truly unique, out of the way, little-known gems, there are a couple websites I like to frequent.

My #1 go-to website is AtlasObscura.com. This site is packed with amazing (and sometimes a little frightening) off-the-wall places that you probably

NEW ORLEANS

wouldn't find anywhere else. For instance, I found an amazing granite statue garden (Victor's Way) in County Wicklow, Ireland, and the Museum of Death in New Orleans! What can I say? I like weird.

Another fun site is CultureTrip.com. This one is a great mix of little-known and better-known attractions around the globe. After living in Nevada for 10 years, I thought I was pretty familiar with its hidden treasures. However, Culture Trip showed me a place called Valley of Fire State Park that I now MUST visit. Red sandstone formed in the time of the dinosaurs! How cool is that?

Another great source for fun sight-seeing adventure ideas is the state or town's own website. For example, our own North Carolina (www.visitnc.com) site has LOADS of great attractions listed, everything from outdoor adventures to museums. Even some of our quilt shops are listed.

Finally, one of the best tips for finding the best things to see and do when out on the road is to ask the locals. Every quilt shop I visit, every museum I check out, I always make a point to ask the employees where they suggest I visit. In fact, I've discovered some of my most favorite hidden gems simply from word of mouth.

A great example was in Virginia. On my last visit to the Mid-Atlantic Quilt Festival near Virginia Beach, I happened to ask one of the locals if they could suggest a fun "artsy type" museum to visit. Their answer? The Hermitage Museum.

This house was spectacular! Purchased in 1908 by William and Florence Sloane, the house started out as a modest 5-room summer cottage and quickly grew to a 42-room mansion and Arts & Crafts museum. Filled with Mrs. Sloane's art and craft collection, stunning architecture, and even a pipe organ, this house is a true gem! Even the lady at the front door helped me choose my next museum stop. The locals know.

Whether you're staying in one city for a quilt show, or shop hopping from town to town, there's always an adventure nearby, if you know where to look.

HERMITAGE COLLECTION

HERMITAGE MUSEUM

HERMITAGE COLLECTION

BARN QUILT IN THE NORTH CAROLINA MOUN

CHAPTER FOUR

Barn Quilt Tours

WHAT ARE BARN QUILT TRAILS?

Donna Sue Groves, whose mother was a quilter, grew up playing the "I-Spy" road trip game, spotting things like barns. When she and her mother later bought a farm in rural Ohio, it had an old ugly tobacco barn on the property. Donna got the idea, in honor of her mother's love of quilting, to paint a pretty quilt block and put it on the side of that barn to make it look a little nicer.

Donna loved the look of that pretty quilt block on the side of the barn so much, she got the idea to create more pretty blocks to beautify more old ugly barns. Eventually, with so many pretty quilt blocks in the area, it made sense to develop a sort of driving tour through her county for families to enjoy the barn quilt art while spending time together.

Her barn quilt tour was a great success! Once word spread, people started coming from all over, including neighboring states, to see the beautiful barn quilts.

With the introduction of that first barn quilt trail by Donna Sue Groves in 2001, both the barn quilts themselves and the idea of barn quilt trails spread like wildfire. Today, you can find them all over the United States, with more popping up every day. You'll find barn quilts not only on barns, but on stores, garages, and even houses. Heck, my next-door neighbor has two. I'd be willing to bet there's one near you as well.

BARN QUILT IN VALLE CRUCIS, NORTH CAROLINA

'65 VETTE

FLORAL CENTERPIECE

BURNSVILLE

EVERY BARN QUILT HAS A STORY

One of the things I enjoy most about finding and photographing barn quilts is learning about their stories. Each one has a reason why it was made and a story about the person who made it.

For instance, a barn quilt called *The 65 'Vette* is very indicative of its location. Mounted on the side of the Burnsville Chevrolet office in Burnsville, North

Carolina, it perfectly portrays what the shop is all about.

Or how about the *Floral Centerpiece* barn quilt: This beautiful barn quilt serves two purposes. Mounted on the side of the Burnsville Florist Shop, the building also houses the fabulous Quilt-N-Code quilt shop. Therefore, this one block represents both the florist and the quilt shop!

Sometimes when I'm out on my travels, I stumble upon something truly unique. That happened not too long ago when I was driving through the back roads here in North Carolina. Out along highway 801 near Graham Road stands a century-old country store. This store is attached to West Rowan Farm and Garden. In addition to being interesting for its age and history, this amazing little building holds a giant community barn quilt that will stop you dead in your tracks.

The entire side of the building is covered in dozens of barn quilt blocks all made by members of the community. Together, they tell the story of the people and its town. These beautiful barn quilt blocks include ones dedicated to cancer survivors, suicide awareness, and even some in memory of those who've passed.

My hope is that more communities can come together to not only celebrate the history and beauty of barn quilts, but also to collectively share their stories through full barn quilt displays just like the one hanging on the side of that little general store.

WHAT IS A BARN QUILT TREASURE HUNT?

A barn quilt tour is more of a treasure hunt, really.

Do you remember going on long road trips and playing the "I-Spy" game just to pass the time?

"I spy with my little eye something… red."

"Is it that quilt on a barn?"

Last fall, I was finally able to convince the hubby to join me on a mountain trip adventure. My husband loves the mountains. However, he's also one of those mission-oriented people. If there's a plan in place, there is no deviating from said plan until the mission is complete. Did I mention he's also prior service Army? However, I am much more of an "Oh look - a giant rooster sign. Let's stop and get a picture!" type of person. Over the years I've come up with some pretty crafty ways of combining both our inclinations.

On this particular road trip, we only had one day for our adventure. But, "What shall we do?" A few months earlier, I had found a *Quilt Trails of Western*

BARN QUILT MAPS

ONE OF A KIND ART GALLERY

ONE OF A KIND ART GALLERY STORE

ONE OF A KIND ART GALLERY STORE

North Carolina driving map at the One-of-a-Kind Art Gallery near Burnsville. That town alone has over 50 barn quilts! I decided to challenge my husband to find as many barn quilts on that map as possible. Thus, our first Barn Quilt Treasure Hunt was born.

Combining our Western North Carolina driving map and the Mt. Mitchell Scenic Byway Quilt Trail map I found online, we began our treasure hunt backwards. Instead of beginning with block #1 as shown on the first map, we started with block #50. Leave it to me to "make things my own." My husband says I just like to do things the hard way. I prefer to think of it as "adding to the adventure."

Either way, we were off! The thing that makes this a true barn quilt treasure hunt is that there are no full addresses to each location. Some include the shop or church name and some include an "on the corner of." But it's up to you and your phone's Google Search to fill in the rest.

HOW TO EXECUTE A BARN QUILT TREASURE HUNT

To properly execute your own barn quilt treasure hunt, you'll need a few essentials:

- Barn Quilt Trail Map
- Google Maps on your cell phone
- Marking Pen (to check off the Barn Quilts you found)
- Camera (You can also use your cell phone)
- A driving partner (or 2 or 3)
- Driving snacks
- And your road trip essentials - (See "What to Pack" in the Shop Hop Road Trips chapter)

Living here in the Carolinas, we are lucky to have several resources for locating barn quilt trail maps. The best site I've found is Quilttrailswnc.org.

However, if you're outside of the Carolinas, you can visit Barnquiltinfo.com to view lists of barn quilt trails in nearly every state of US. Also, a quick Google search for "Barn Quilt Trails" in your neck of the woods should yield a website or two where you can locate your local barn quilt trail maps.

Planning a barn quilt tour can actually be hit or miss. This is because some maps are outdated and don't include some barn quilts being removed and others added. However, as long as you can find your starting position, you should be able to follow along. After all, a little hunting is what makes this a treasure hunt, right?

When looking at your map, it's good to decide how long you want to be on the road. For us, we knew we only wanted to spend one day, so our "hunting grounds" were limited. Depending on the number of barn quilts and how spread out they are, you can plan to drive about 30 - 50 miles of a barn quilt tour per day.

This may sound like not a long distance. However, keep in mind you will be doing a lot of stopping to take pictures and slow driving to find those elusive barn quilts that may or may not be where the map says they should be. Plus, there will be added driving time to get to and from the barn quilt trail area.

When figuring out your driving time, it's also a good idea to add in at least 1 hour for lunch. Even if you decide to pack a picnic lunch, you'll more than likely want to pull over somewhere to enjoy your meal.

WHILE ON YOUR DRIVE

While on the trip, you can use your Google Maps application's search function to find the address of your first barn quilt treasure hunt stop, or you can try to find another building close by.

For us, our first stop was the *Cross and Crown,* mounted on the Bald Creek Methodist Church. Unfortunately, the church did not show up on our Google Maps GPS search.

However, the Bald Creek Elementary school on the same road did. So, we followed the GPS to the school and guess what? Not only was the Church half a block away, but the school had a barn quilt too!

Of course, if you're a little old fashioned like me, you can also use your trusty old hard copy AAA maps. Yes, I still use those too. If you have a AAA membership, the maps are free and you can get them either inside a local AAA office or on their website at AAA.com.

The most important thing in any treasure hunt, whether it be a traditional or a barn quilt treasure hunt, is to just have fun. Make it a relaxing afternoon with friends and/or family and enjoy the art, the scenery, and most especially, the company!

BALD CREEK ELEMENTARY

BALD CREEK METHODIST CHURCH

PONDEROSA
QUILT RETREAT
CENTER

CHAPTER FIVE

Quilting Retreats

WHAT IS A QUILT RETREAT?

The informal gathering of crafters is as old as time. Much of those gatherings were born of necessity. For instance, after the invention of the loom, most people could not afford to purchase one for their home not to mention have the room to store the loom when not in use. So, some communities would come together to purchase a communal loom.

In the fall, after the harvest, the entire townsfolk, young and old, boys and girls, would all come together to sit and get crafting. The large loom would be set up outside due to its size and to allow the weaver to better see the reeds when threading. Houses back then didn't have many windows and were only lit by candle-light.

Because it would take 8 spinners to keep up with 1 person working the loom, everyone pitched in. Some would be cleaning the wool and linen, some would work the spinning wheels, and one would work the loom. All to make sure each household had enough yarn and fabric to make clothing, blankets, etc. for the coming winter.

THE OLDEST LOOM IN U.S. AT HICKORY RIDGE

You've heard the term "whistle while you work?" Well, these towns-people would talk and gossip and teach and enjoy each other's company while they toiled away, yard

HICKORY RIDGE SPINDLE

CROSSNORE WEAVERS

after yard, spool after spool. Talk about knowing everyone's business. I'm pretty sure no one could hide from the gossip mills in those days!

Many things have changed since that time. Today we have electric sewing machines and rows upon rows of fabrics and thread to choose from at our local quilt shops. However, the one thing that hasn't changed is the joy we get from getting together in a room to work on our craft.

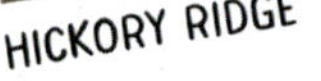

HICKORY RIDGE

Enter the quilting retreat.

In its truest definition, a quilting retreat is merely a group of quilters getting together in a room for any length of time to quilt. These gatherings could be for one day or one week. They could be at a quilter's house or in a fancy hotel conference room. Heck, they can even be on a cruise ship! More on that in a few chapters.

More specifically, a quilting retreat is a magical place where you get to leave the world, and everyone in it, behind for just a few days to focus on meeting new people, sharing quilting stories, laughing, eating, and SEWING! Did I mention there's lots of sewing? Oh yea, and there's more sewing. In fact, there's so much sewing that one could realistically finish several projects in just a few days.

Picture it: You're sitting at a quilting table with nothing but your machine, fabric, and favorite quilting supplies. There's no family to ask when dinner will be ready. No dog that needs walking. No laundry that needs tending. No boss that needs that TPS report like yesterday. There's nothing but you, your machine, and a handful of like-minded individuals all working on fabulous works of fabric art. Just heavenly.

WHERE CAN I FIND A QUILTING RETREAT?

Some of my favorite stories from my grandmother were about her and her sisters getting together when one of them finished a quilt top. All the girls would meet at one of their houses, set up the giant quilting hoop, and they'd all get to work. Hands would fly and mouths would run. Oh yes, this was the time they would all swap new recipes and gossip about who was doing what where and with whom. But oh, those quilts!

If you're interested in attending a quilting retreat, the best place to start looking for one is at your local quilters' guild. Many times, the guilds themselves will organize an annual retreat for their members. Also, a good place to look would be your local quilt shops. If the shops themselves do not organize retreats, they may have flyers or know of websites you can go to find one.

If you are interested in taking a larger quilting retreat, a good place to look is Missouri Star Quilting Company (www.missouriquiltco.com). They hold several quilting retreats in their hometown of Hamilton, Missouri, all year long. In fact, owner Jenny Doan and her daughters lead many of them in person! But be sure to sign up for those well in advance, because they sell out very quickly.

Finally, you can always do a Google search for quilting retreats. If you go that route, however, make sure to look carefully at who is organizing the retreat and where the quilting retreat is being held. You definitely don't want to sign up for a super fun looking quilting retreat only to find out that it's being held in England. Unless, of course, you're in the market to travel to Europe!

WHAT TO EXPECT AT A QUILTING RETREAT

For the most part, there are two main types of quilt retreats: ones where each participant brings their own quilt projects to work on, and those where an instructor is hired to teach a particular project and/or technique to the group. I personally love both!

As for the specifics of each quilt retreat, that will depend on where the quilt retreat is being held. Technically speaking, they can be held just about anywhere. However, for our purposes here, let's focus on those quilt retreats that are formally organized.

Sewing Space

Most organized quilt retreats will be held in an actual quilt retreat center. This is usually a large house, or something similar, that has been fitted to solely accommodate quilters. At the retreat center, you will find everything you would in an average house, such as a kitchen, bathrooms, bedrooms, etc. However, the general living spaces are set up with quilting tables, cutting, and ironing stations. Many retreat centers will also have design walls you can use!

Once you arrive, you will be assigned a designated quilting area. This will be

PONDEROSA QUILT RETREAT CENTER

your "home away from home" sewing space. And more than likely, you won't have to move throughout the duration of your quilt retreat. So spread out and get comfy, because you have a lot of quilting to do, my friend!

Sleeping Accommodations

As I mentioned, most quilting retreat centers are big houses. Therefore, in order to fit in as many people as possible, you will most likely be sharing a room. If you have a quilting friend or two who also want to go to the quilt retreat, you should be able to share the room together. Just be sure to tell the host who is in your party when you make your reservation.

I've seen retreat centers accommodate anywhere from 2 to 5 people per room, depending on the size. Even if you get to share a room with a new quilting friend, you probably won't be spending too much time in there. Generally, the majority of your time will be spent quilting!

RELAXATION

FELLOWSHIP

QUILTING!

Food

I love to eat. And because I'm not too picky of an eater, I love to eat almost any type of food. Since eating arrangements are handled differently at each quilt retreat, I try to find ones where I don't have to cook!

MAKING USE OF EVERY SPACE!

Most quilting retreats will have some sort of food plan set up for your stay. Some will have a cook on staff. Some will even have the quilt retreat professionally catered. And there are some that will have an open kitchen and ask the guests to cook their own meals.

The meal sharing thing can be hit or miss. If you get a group of quilters that also love to cook, you can get some pretty great meals! However, if you get a group that doesn't like to cook, or only cooks things you can't/won't eat, you might end up going out to eat. Therefore, it's always a good idea to find out how the food accommodations are handled before you sign up for a quilt retreat.

✈ **PRO TIP:** *If you have any kind of special food allergies or preferences, be sure to mention them to the quilt retreat host when you first register. This way they have plenty of time to make preparations for you.*

HOW MUCH DOES A QUILTING RETREAT COST?

The cost for quilt retreats can vary based on several factors, such as the location, duration, and whether or not there will be an instructor present. However, generally you can expect to pay anywhere between $100 - $600 for a full quilt retreat.

There are a few things to consider when you're pricing out a quilt retreat to get a better rate. The first is the length of stay.

Most quilt retreats can last between 2 and 4 nights. This will include nearly non-stop sewing, which, as glorious as it sounds, can be incredibly exhausting. My tushy hurts just thinking about 4 days of straight sewing. Plus, if you have lower back issues or tend to get stiff after long periods at the sewing table, you may want to look for a shorter retreat.

The second factor is the type of quilt retreat. The retreats that host an instructor are almost always going to be more expensive. Plus, they will more than likely be teaching a project or technique during your stay as well. If the instructor is one you like or the project interests you, I definitely recommend grabbing your spot. But if you're like me (and so many others) and have stacks of UFO's (Unfinished projects), then an "open sew" quilt retreat might be more your cup of tea.

UFO'S IN PROGRESS

WHAT TO PACK FOR A QUILT RETREAT?

So you've just signed up for your first quilt retreat. Now comes the most important question: "What do I pack?!"

First, don't panic. The best way to figure out what you need to take with you on a quilt retreat is to check with the host. When you register for a quilt retreat, the host should provide you with a complete list of what they do and don't provide. If it is a project-based quilt retreat, there should be a supply list provided as well.

However, here are a few key things to also verify with the host beforehand:

- Will the bed linens be provided? (Some retreat centers require you to bring your own)
- Will there be cutting stations set up for use?

- Will there be plenty of full-size irons and ironing boards available?
- How much sewing space will be available? (one person to a table or sharing?)
- What type of sewing chairs will we be using? (you may want to bring a tushy or back pillow)
- What meals and/or snacks will be provided?
- What other amenities are available on the grounds of the retreat center/ facility?

A good quilt retreat host should be able to answer all of these questions for you as well as any others you may have. This way, you'll be well prepared to have everything you'll need once you arrive.

> ✈ **PRO** *TIP: Be sure to write your name on all of your quilting supplies so there's no confusion if supplies get shared or moved around. This way all the supplies you brought with you also make it safely back home.*

Now let's talk about transportation of supplies. You will need to bring a lot of supplies to really enjoy your relaxing quilt retreat. Believe me, there's nothing worse

than having nearly a full day left in the retreat and you've just finished the only project you brought. That's why I now bring more projects than I even think I can finish, because when you have zero interruptions, you'd be amazed at what you can accomplish!

Lots of supplies means lots of bags. Well, sort of. Yes, I even have a few packing tricks for quilt retreats. What can I say? I love a good jigsaw puzzle.

First, get yourself a good suitcase for your sewing machine. But don't take your big bulky sewing machine. Now, I fully understand if you only own one machine and that's fine. However, if you can, I highly recommend getting yourself a nice smaller, lighter weight sewing machine that you can use specifically for travel. I have an old Brother machine that I've had for years. It's a workhorse, small enough to travel with, but strong enough to get through just about any quilt project.

✈ **PRO TIP:** *Whichever machine you use to start one project, use the same machine to finish it. Many machines have slightly different settings for the ¼ inch mark as well as timing, etc. so your blocks may be completely different if sewn on different machines.*

Next, get comfortable with stuffing your machine. Ok, I totally just made a sewing machine sound like a turkey. Not my intention, but here we are. Basically, in order to make use of all available space, I like to stuff my fabric and other items in and around my sewing machine inside its suitcase. You can stuff everything from batting to your notion kits to basting spray. If it fits... well, you know.

✈ **PRO TIP:** *If you have more than one set of quilting supplies, you can keep one set stored with your travel sewing machine. That way, when your next sewing travel opportunity arrives, you'll already be nearly packed and ready to go.*

Finally, your personal bag. I treat this one like I do my carry-on bags for airline travel. Pack super comfy clothes (lots of sewing, yes?), only what you NEED, and make sure to roll your clothes to save space. It's likely you will not be leaving the quilting retreat location until it's time to head home. So be sure to bring clothes that you'd normally wear to sit around and sew all day.

However, I should mention that you will be sewing around other humans and there is the possibility of heading to a restaurant and/or a local quilt shop once or twice, so make sure you have at least one pair of real shoes and don't forget to put on pants. Ok, that one may just be a reminder for me.

CLIFFS OF MOHER

CHAPTER SIX

Quilt Tours

WHAT ARE QUILT TOURS?

Have you ever had an itch to see the world but don't want to go alone? Did you know there are several tour groups that do just that and are geared specifically for quilters? Hundreds of quilt tours are scheduled each year to places like Ireland, England, Japan, Egypt, Iceland, and even many quilt destinations here in the United States.

A few years ago, master quilter Mark Sherman came to speak at our local quilters guild and brought with him some flyers. He was advertising his first quilt tour to Ireland with Craft Tours. On that trip, he would be premiering his amazing *Book of Kells* quilt at Trinity College in Dublin and teaching a series of short quilt workshops. On a whim, I picked up a flyer and took it home.

The next day, I showed the flyer to my husband and half-jokingly told him we should go. No way did I expect the next words out of his mouth: "When do you leave?"

Dumbfounded that my husband, Mr. "Why do we need to spend money on that" was encouraging me to go to Ireland on a quilt tour. I quickly hopped on the phone and made my reservation before he decided to rethink his position.

That trip changed my life. Seriously. Twelve strangers from various parts of the US came together in New York to trek across the Atlantic and explore just a few of the amazing sights and experiences Ireland has to offer. After 9 days, those strangers left as lifelong friends. It was, by far, one of the best trips I've ever taken.

WHY A QUILT TOUR?

For over 30 years, a handful of tour companies have been taking quilters of all ages and skill levels to various locations around the world. These traveling quilters get to experience quilt shops, retreats, shows, and much more.

CLIFFS OF MOHER ARE A LITTLE WINDY

There are definitely a few pros and cons to going on an organized quilt tour. The biggest pros:

Everything is done for you. Once you sign up, all that's required is for you to show up and enjoy. All of your accommodations, travel, ticketing, and itinerary has been scheduled for you.

New friends! Going in, you already know that everyone on your trip is a fellow quilter. That means you already have something in common. By the end of the trip, you'll all be great friends who have experienced a grand adventure together.

Security and peace of mind. There's safety in numbers. That fact, coupled with your tour guides and their expertise, can help you feel safe and secure to better enjoy your trip.

The only potential drawback that I can see with organized Quilt tours might be the price.

WHAT TO EXPECT ON A QUILT TOUR

Each quilt tour is unique. They vary in size and destination. Some schedule all your meal locations. Others only schedule a few. Some include full quilt workshops and others do not. Some will take you to various quilt shops, while others don't include a stop at a single one. However, the biggest thing you can expect on every quilt tour is to be traveling with an entire group of fellow quilters.

CAHIR CASTLE,
CO. TIPPERARY,
IRELAND

For me, I always feel comforted going into a quilt tour because right away I know we all have a significant common interest. And, if you're like me, you can talk about quilting 'til the cows come home. It's sort of like a great unifier amongst people who might otherwise be strangers.

The next thing to expect is that the group will be filled with all sorts of interesting personalities. There will be the super adventurous one who would rather be exploring when she should really be napping (that's usually me). There might also be the "Auntie Mame" type that keeps the entire group laughing. There usually will also be the shy one who isn't really sure what to say to strike up a conversation. These are the people I like to seek out first to make them feel welcome and part of the group.

No matter who you meet, you're sure to find lifelong friends after experiencing such a wonderful adventure together.

Whether your goal is to see the US or to see the world, there is a quilt tour adventure out there waiting for you. From workshops to tours, museums to the wild outdoors, it's sure to be the quilting adventure of a lifetime!

WHAT DOES A QUILT TOUR COST?

As a general standard, full 1 – 2 week long quilt tours can range from $1,000 up to $5,000 per person, depending on the duration and the destination. However, most of them offer payment plans so you can spread the expense out a bit.

I know that may seem like a large chunk of change; however, consider what is included in the price:

- All entrance fees to exhibits, museums, etc. that are part of the itinerary
- Hotel accommodations and scheduling
- All transportation costs while on the tour
- A professional tour guide
- Some tours include a quilting workshop with established quilt teacher
- Most include some meals
- Many also include airfare to and from your tour destination

ALWAYS TAKE THE COOKING CLASS!

I've also seen quilt tours that offer special "behind the scenes" type adventures that you can only experience with a tour group.

WHAT TO PACK ON A QUILT TOUR

Before going to Ireland, I had absolutely no idea what to take with me. I checked the weather projections so that I could pack appropriate clothing. Then, I bought a brand-new pair of walking shoes. If you do this, please make sure you break them in for at least 2 weeks BEFORE your trip. Your feet will thank you.

However, when it came to the size of my bag or the type of carry-on or even the quilting supplies I might need, I was clueless. So, I just bought the biggest suitcase I could find and filled it with whatever I THOUGHT I might need. I'm here to tell you, I didn't even need half of what I brought. In fact, I ended up leaving a few things in Ireland.

For most quilt tours, especially overseas, you will be doing a lot of moving around. Unlike quilt retreats where you mostly stay in one building, on quilt tours you'll most likely be staying at a few different hotels and traveling to many different cities. I grant you that tour buses do have a decent size storage area. Unfortunately, **you** will be the one lugging that bag around to and from each hotel change.

So to save your back and your sanity, I highly suggest going with a medium-size suitcase that is on wheels.

For 1 week of travel, here is what I suggest you pack:

- 3 shirts
- 2 pairs of pants
- 1 pair of shorts for warmer climates
- 1 pair of good walking shoes
- Bathroom products kit (travel-size bottles)
- Any medications required for the full length of your quilt tour
- Light rain jacket that can squish into your day bag
- Regular jacket for colder climates
- 1 - 2 items and/or projects to keep you busy during down times. For this I highly suggest a hand quilting project, a smaller-sized book, or perhaps an electronic tablet for playing games or watching movies.

✈ **PRO TIP:** *To save space in your luggage, roll your clothes instead of folding them. This technique has been used by military personnel for generations to fit all their gear inside one duffel bag.*

To save space and time, there are a few things I recommend you leave at home:

Laptop. As useful as they are, laptops can be heavy and take up a lot of room, especially when you add in their cords and mouse. However, if you have one, an electronic tablet would be a much better space-saving option.

Full-size bathroom product bottles. These are bulky and you will not need that much product for such a short time of travel.

Too many projects. On your tour, you will have very little down time. Therefore, the only projects you should need are things to keep you busy on the plane and/or at night before bed.

GETTING IT ALL HOME

With most quilt tours, there are 2 different types of "carry-on" baggage. One refers to the bag you carry on board an airplane to meet your group. The other refers to the day bag you'll carry on the bus along your journey. Over the years, I've developed a unique trick to using these various bags to make the most of your limited space and save on baggage fees.

For my quilt tour travels, whether domestic or international, I take 3 pieces of luggage: My medium suitcase (on wheels), a duffel bag/backpack, and my favorite travel purse.

When I first pack to head out on the quilt tour, I will roll the empty duffel bag and pack it INSIDE my medium suitcase. As long as I keep the clothing

A TOAST TO IRELAND!

GALWAY

CATHEDRAL OF GALWAY

KYLEMORE ABBEY

rolled tight and my "extras" to a minimum, the duffel fits just fine.

For my carry-on, I simply bring my travel purse. Inside it fits perfectly my cell phone, travel documents, my little purse kit (see "What to Pack" in the Shop Hops chapter) and a ziptop bag filled with my latest English Paper Piecing project. As I also love to read on planes, there is a Kindle application on my phone. However, a small book will also fit inside my travel purse.

Now, here is where I should confess that I tend to purchase entirely too many goodies while on my travels. For instance, I collect keychains and shot glasses. Plus, I like to bring trinkets home as gifts for my family, and of course, FABRIC! Oh yes, that alluring call of cotton gets me every time.

Unfortunately, my shopping fun tends to take up quite a bit of room in my suitcase. So, this is where the duffel bag comes in.

While packing to make the trip home, I will pack my rolled clothes and anything that can be carried on board an airplane inside the duffel bag. Then, I fill my suitcase with all my purchased treasures and anything that must be checked (like whiskey for my husband). The suitcase gets checked and the duffel becomes my carry on. This way I can still get everything home without having to pay to check a second bag or bring one that is just too large to manage.

If you do not have a duffel bag to bring, or you go a little overboard on your purchases (haven't we all), there is always the option to have your items shipped. Many of the shops will have the option to do this for you. For instance, when we were at Avoca Mill in Ireland they offered to ship any of our bulky woolen items back to the States for us.

BLACK FACE SHEEP HAVE NO FEAR

FRESH HONEY AT OUR HOTEL

WORRY TREE

When taking advantage of this option, keep in mind there may be an added fee and there should be someone at home to receive the package so it doesn't sit on your porch until your return.

Whether you purchase an extra suitcase full or nothing at all, whether you are touring the backwoods of Georgia or the geysers of Iceland, whether you're with a group of 12 or a group of 30, your quilt tour is sure to be one of the best quilting adventures of a lifetime!

LOOM AT AVOCA WOOLEN MILL, CO. WICKLOW

BEACH TIME IN BONAIRE

CHAPTER SEVEN

Quilt Cruises

WHAT IS A QUILT CRUISE?

Arguably, one of the best things about a quilt retreat is the days of uninterrupted sewing. Days where you can just sew for hours and hours surrounded by several of your fellow quilting enthusiasts. Also, one of the best things about a quilt tour is getting to explore the world while enjoying the fellowship of even more amazing quilting enthusiasts.

So, what happens when you put both a quilt retreat and quilt tour together? You take them for a boat ride!

Cruising has been around for ages. With multiple destinations all over the globe, the excitement of boarding a ship for fun and adventure on the high seas calls many a man and woman. Over the years the boats have gotten bigger (MUCH bigger) and the adventures have gotten even more grand. Some even have a theme. Enter the quilt cruise.

EXPLORER OF THE SEAS

I love history and researching random facts about various things. However, as hard as I tried, I could not find exactly when the first quilt cruise took place. The earliest reference I located was mention of a group of quilters taking a cruise in 2008. Somehow, I feel like that was not the first quilt cruise.

Either way, my hat is off to whoever those first quilters were who got the brilliant idea to take their quilting prowess to the high seas.

Today there are a handful of quilt cruise companies (and a few quilt shops) that organize quilt cruises. These cruises travel literally all over the globe. You could travel through Germany on a river boat cruise, around the Panama Canal, spend a week sailing around the Caribbean, or even take a whirlwind excursion around Europe. And those are just a few of the many, many quilt cruise destination options.

HOW MUCH DOES A QUILT CRUISE COST?

There are several things that will determine the cost of a quilt cruise. Things like the cruise ship, destination, duration, and which teachers will be teaching which project. However, on average you can expect to pay between $1,000 and $4,000 for a quilt cruise.

So, what is included in the price? Quite a lot, actually! On most quilt cruises, you can expect the following items to be included in the cost.

- All shipboard accommodations
- Almost all shipboard meals and entertainment

READY FOR THE QUILTERS

- Port of call fees
- Stateroom
- Quilting workshops on all "at sea" days and most nights
- Sewing machines to use
- Sewing machine technical assistance to help you use your machines and keep you sewing with little interruption
- Open sewing time on "off hours" to work on whatever project you wish
- Private quilters-only events
- Demos and/or "make and take" events

And sometimes more!

Tons of great stuff, right? Now let's talk a bit about the items that are NOT included in the price.

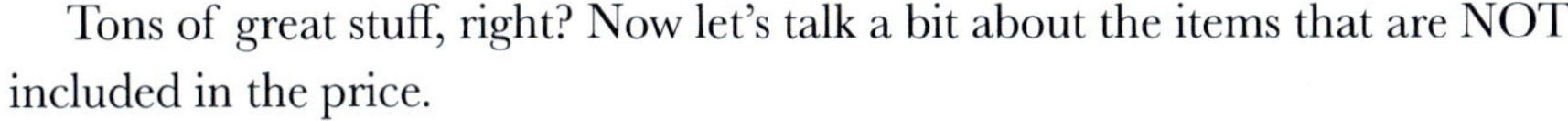

On most cruise lines all the food is included. However, some ships have a few restaurants where you'll have to pay separately. Also, you'll need to purchase a "drink card" for sodas and alcohol.

One pretty great thing the cruise lines have done is to create a keycard program for their cruisers. Once you first check in, you'll be issued a "ship pass" that is registered to your room. All necessary purchases will be charged to that card. It's similar to how things work at most hotels these days when you charge things to your hotel room.

Kit fees: When you book your quilt cruise, be sure to ask about the kit fee(s) for your workshop(s). Some quilt cruise companies will include the kit fees in the price of the quilt cruise. Others will not. It's better to know what to expect up front.

Finally, here's a list of the remaining items generally NOT covered in the price of your quilt cruise.

- Passport fees
- Airfare
- Transportation to and from the ship
- Shore excursions

Whenever you are in doubt, always ask your quilt cruise company agent. They should be able to go over all the payment details and answer any questions you may have.

WHAT TO EXPECT ON A QUILT CRUISE

I have to be honest. Quilt cruising is the one quilt travel topics I know the least about. So I reached out to a few of my fellow quilt teachers and quilting travelers that have much more experience in this arena. And thanks to all of their amazing knowledge and experience, I feel super confident in all the information I'm about to share with you. In fact, I feel so confident, it almost feels like I took all of those quilt cruises with them!

The average quilt cruise lasts around 7 – 10 days. However, I've seen some that are as long as 12 days. During that time, you will have "at sea" days and "port days." The "at sea" days are your quilting days. These are the days where you will get to attend your quilt classes, usually between 9 AM and 4 PM with a nice lunch break in between. Many quilt cruises will leave the sewing rooms open 24 hours so you can continue sewing to your heart's content.

Your "port" days are the days where the ship docks and you get the option of going on shore for an organized excursion or to just look around on your own. I'll provide a few important points about these shore excursions a little later.

The first thing you need to know when looking for a quilt cruise is which quilt cruise you want to take. With so many options out there, it can be hard to decide which one is right for you. Therefore, I highly suggest basing your final choice on 3 things: the destination, the teacher, and the project. Not necessarily in that order.

Personally, the destination would be the first on my list. You may want to go to someplace you've never been before. The reason for this is the great off-ship excursions you can choose to add on.

At each port of call (or stopping point) along the quilt cruise, you will have the option to disembark (get off the ship) and take a mini adventure on land.

LOBSTER IN MAINE AT BEAL'S LOBSTER POUND

MAKING BATIK

PRIVATE TOUR OF CARABELLA ST. KITTS

DOWNTOWN CURACAO

Some quilt cruise companies even offer shore excursions of their own, which may include visits to quilt shops or even a batik factory tour!

The next thing to look at is the teacher(s) and the projects being offered. Each quilt cruise is totally unique. However, the one thing they all have in common is a quilt workshop (or two or three). Some quilt cruises will have only 1 teacher who will be teaching one project. Other cruises may have as many as 3 teachers offering 3 different classes.

I do want to mention quickly here that most of the quilt classes offered on quilt cruises are designed for quilters that already know the basics. Of course, all skill level of quilters are welcome! I just want to make sure that if you are a brand new quilter, you know there may be a slight learning curve.

✈ **PRO TIP:** *If you have to fly to meet the ship at its departure location, always book your flight for the day BEFORE you leave. Delayed flights due to weather or other factors can force people to miss their quilt cruise departure if they cut it too close. You can usually find decent hotels near the port to stay the night. This way, you can be rested and arrive in plenty of time to make your quilt cruise departure the next morning.*

✈ **BONUS TIP:** *ALWAYS get the travel insurance. As I mentioned in the "International Travel" and "Quilt Tour" chapters, it's better to have the insurance and not need it than to need it and not have it. For most quilt cruises, the insurance will not only cover any accidents and lost or stolen items, but it also covers unforeseen cancellations.*

VIEW FROM CABIN
ON THE ALLURE

SHORE EXCURSIONS

If you choose to take a shore excursion, there are few key points to remember. And I can't stress these enough!

1. Book your shore excursions early as they will probably sell out. Most cruise lines will allow you to book a shore excursion up to 90 days in advance. Your quilt cruise company travel agent should be able to help you find out more about what shore excursions will be offered and how to register.

2. Only take a shore excursion organized by the cruise line or your quilt cruise company. If your trip back to the ship is delayed for any reason and you are not with a cruise-organized tour group, the ship WILL leave you behind.

3. If you decide to spend the day by yourself exploring the area, make sure to be back to the ship in plenty of time to re-board. The ship will tell you what time to be back. Keep in mind that the lines to get back on board can be very long.

4. Make a point to find out if the ship is running on "local time" or "ship time." Local time is the time zone of the current port you are in. Ship time refers to the time zone of your original port of departure. For instance, if you began your cruise in Florida, the ship time would be US Eastern time (GMT -5).

✈ **PRO TIP:** *Most cell phones are programmed to automatically change their time to whichever time zone you are located. Therefore, before you disembark the ship for your shore excursion, figure out what the "back on-board time" is in the local time zone, then set an alarm on your cell phone so that you get back to the ship in plenty of time before it leaves. Once again, if you are not back on board in time, the ship WILL leave without you.*

WHAT TO PACK ON A QUILT CRUISE

You've decided on your quilt cruise and now you're ready to get packed. But what do you need to take with you?

Quilting Supplies

Most cruise ships were not specifically designed for quilting. Therefore, the quilting classes are usually held in the onboard conference rooms. Some of these rooms can hold 15 people. Some can accommodate up to 40. Therefore, your class sizes will vary as well. On average, you can expect about 30 people per class.

When you arrive for your class, you'll be assigned a sewing station. The sewing machine will already be waiting for you. This will be your machine and your spot for the duration of the quilt cruise. If there are 3 teachers in 3 different conference rooms, they will rotate around you. Unlike classes at a quilt show where you drag all your supplies from room to room, on a quilt cruise, the teachers are the ones room-hopping.

As for the fabric needed for your quilt projects, most of the teachers will supply full kits for you to use. Also, many will have more kits and fabric available for an additional purchase.

All in all, the only real quilting supplies you'll need to bring with you on board your quilt cruise is in your basic quilting kit. The full list of specific items required will be given to you with your registration paperwork.

✈ **PRO TIP:** *Just like when you travel to a quilt retreat write your name on all of your quilting supplies in permanent marker. That way, there will be no guessing what belongs to whom in the sewing rooms.*

Irons and Rotary Cutters

In the quilt cruise world, irons, rotary cutters, blades, and large scissors are technically "prohibited." In fact, you are not allowed to bring power strips or large irons on board a cruise ship at all. The electricity capacity is limited. However, you are allowed to bring a small travel-size craft iron (400-watt capacity or less) on board. A few large irons will be provided by the quilt cruise staff for use during the classes.

This next little trick I learned from the fabulous ladies over at Stitchin' Heaven in Texas. The easiest way to take your prohibited items on board is to pack them in a gallon-size ziptop bag. Using a permanent marker, write your room number and your reservation or group number on the bag. Then place it in your CARRY-ON bag.

Your suitcase luggage will be collected by a porter on shore and taken to your room. Therefore, you will need a smaller bag, or your purse, that you will hand carry on board with you. This is where you will place your ziptop bag.

I know this may sound counterintuitive. However, if you placed the items in your suitcase, security will definitely flag it as containing prohibited items. Your suitcase would then be sent to their security office for further inspection and your bags could be delayed by a full day or 2 before they get delivered to your room.

Conversely, if you have them in your carry-on bag and they get flagged by security, you are there to explain what they will be used for. And, as a worst-case

CLASSTIME

scenario, if security does take them, they will be delivered to the conference room and be waiting for you there. No delay in your suitcases being delivered to your room.

Clothes

On most cruise line commercials, you see people dressed up in fancy clothes at night to go to dinner or to see a show on board. I'm here to tell you this is false advertising. The only real requirements for dining are that you are fully dressed and have on shoes. No one cares if you wear your jeans and t-shirt to the lunch buffet.

However, you are required to wear long pants for dinner. Basically, you want to wear something you'd wear on "date night" with your spouse to your favorite local restaurant. Of course, if you want to get all gussied up for dinner, go for it! I mean, how often do you get to wear your best dress?

During your sewing days and on shore, I'd bring comfortable clothes. Depending on the climate you're traveling to, you may want to bring shorts and t-shirts for shore excursions and a swimsuit for hanging out by the pool. Or, if you're on something like an Alaska cruise, you may want to bring long pants and a jacket. Of course, when in doubt, your travel agent should be able to help you decide.

✈ **PRO TIP:** *Don't over-pack your suitcase(s). When you pack your suitcase to leave for your quilt cruise, remember that you will be bringing home the quilt project you've been working on and possibly several souvenirs and other goodies picked up along the way. Especially if you are flying to and from the port of call, you will have to allow for space to transport all those items back home.*

To avoid paying the extra baggage fees, you can also use my duffel bag packing trick from the "What to Pack on a Quilting Tour" section.

✈ **BONUS TIP:** *The night before you leave the ship for the last time, you will be asked to pack your suitcase(s) and hand them off to the porters or leave them in the hallway. Be sure to keep a full change of clothes with you for the next day! There have been several instances of a few embarrassed folks having to depart in their pajamas.*

FREQUENTLY ASKED QUESTIONS

In all honesty, I could write for days on the topic of quilt cruises. There's just so much information to share. However, to save your time and mine, here are a few of the most frequently-asked questions about quilt cruises.

Do I need a passport?

Yes. Most quilt cruises are either traveling to an international destination (like Europe or the Caribbean) or, at the very least, will be traveling through international waters. Therefore, it's a good idea to have your passport just in case.

✈ **PRO TIP:** *Having a passport book is much better and easier than a passport card.*

Are payment plans offered?

Yes. Almost all of the quilt cruise travel companies offer some form of payment plan for your quilt cruise.

What if I'm traveling alone?

No problem at all. You have 2 options. First, you can pay a little more for a single room. Or, you can have the travel company pair you with another solo traveler.

When I took the quilt tour to Ireland in 2017, I was a solo traveler. Luckily, there was also another solo traveler they were able to pair me with.

A SPECIAL COCKTAIL PARTY

ARUBA

MY ROOMIE IN IRELAND

QUILT CRUISE PHOTOS PROVIDED BY DAWN OLMSTEAD WITH QUILT AND CRUISE

Several months before the tour began, we were given each other's contact information. That gave us a chance to get to know each other well in advance of having to share a room together. By the time we finally met in person it was like I was rooming with an old friend. And, all these years later, we are still great friends!

Can I bring my spouse / non-quilting friend

Absolutely! Although I should throw in a caveat here. Spouses and non-quilting friends are always welcome on any cruise. However, make sure they are OK with spending lots of time on their own. During the "at sea" days, you will be spending all day quilting without them. That said, on some quilt cruises, the non-quilting spouses/friends/family members have often formed their own little groups and become fast friends as well!

As I mentioned previously, if you ever have any doubt or questions concerning taking a quilt cruise, the best thing to do is ask the quilt cruise company travel agent. They have all the nitty-gritty details you could ever need. Plus, it's their job to make sure you get the most from your fabulous quilt cruise adventure!

CHAPTER EIGHT

Travel Safety Tips

SAFETY ON THE ROAD

Who doesn't love a road trip? Any excuse to get out of the house and explore new areas, new sights, new sounds. But what if fear is holding you back? One of the top concerns I hear preventing some from traveling more is safety. This is especially true when traveling alone.

However, as I'm quite frequently a solo traveler, I've found that a little bit of preparation goes a long way in the fear department. Knowing you have a plan is the best way to set your mind at ease and get you out on the open road.

What to Pack

The first thing in road trip safety preparation is packing for the "what ifs." My grandfather used to always carry a safety bag in his trunk wherever he went. In fact, when he passed many years ago and I inherited his car, that emergency pack was still in the trunk. And even though I've made a few upgrades and updates, that pack still remains in my trunk today.

✈ **BONUS TIP:** *If you do a lot of road trips, I highly suggest joining a car club. My husband and I have been members of AAA for at least 20 years, and every year the membership has paid for itself: everything from needing a replacement truck battery in the middle of the night to needing an emergency tow while broken down in the middle of a busy highway.*

Literally, the front passenger side wheel decided to pop off just as I was traveling in the center lane where two interstates merged together. There was no shoulder on that particular section and even if there were, with a dislocated

QUILT INSPIRATION IS EVERYWHERE

wheel, the car wasn't moving.

I was alone in the car, so after calming myself down, I called 911 to have them send a patrol car to help alert people I was there. Then, I called AAA. That's probably the only time I was happy to have flashing lights behind me! AAA put a rush on the order and a tow truck was there in 30 minutes. AAA, the driver, and the police officer were my lifesavers that day.

Before You Hit The Road

The second thing on my road trip safety checklist is getting the car serviced. Before a big trip, I always take my car in to get an oil change. I also make sure to let my mechanic know that I'm heading out for a road trip. That way, he'll give the vehicle an extra "once-over." You want them to check all the basics:

- Tire pressure
- All fluid levels
- Air filter
- All lights and blinkers
- Car Battery

The one time I didn't get my battery checked before a trip I was on my way to Georgia. I made it halfway through South Carolina when my battery completely died. The car wouldn't start. Once again, it was AAA to the rescue. A quick battery change and I was on the road. However, if I had just had it checked before I left, it would have saved me that extra time and extra battery fee.

On the Road

Once your road trip safety pack is in the trunk and the all-clear is given on your vehicle, it's time to hit the road. Here are a few things to keep in mind as you travel.

1. NEVER RUN OUT OF FUEL

I like to start looking for a gas station about the time my car's gas indicator reaches 1/4 tank. The last thing you want is to run out of fuel in the middle of nowhere.

AAA TO THE RESCUE!

Another good habit to get into when on longer drives is to ask how many miles until the next fueling opportunity. This is especially helpful if you're in the mountains or on an open road in the desert.

2. KEEP YOUR DOORS LOCKED

When you stop in to check out that cute new quilt shop or pull in for a museum stop, make sure to keep your doors locked and your valuables out of sight.

Once my friend and I ran into a fast-food place to grab a quick order to go. We took our wallets but left our purses in the car. Even though we were gone less than 10 minutes, it was enough time for someone to break the window and rummage through our purses. From then on, I always hide my purse or anything that might look valuable in the trunk before heading indoors.

3. ALWAYS BE AWARE OF YOUR SURROUNDINGS

This one is especially true at gas pumps. When you fuel up, do you grab your charge card and leave your purse and wallet in the passenger seat? Do you lock that door? Most people don't. Thieves have been known to pull into the next pump over and sneakily open the car's passenger doors, take the purse/wallet, and leave. It may be a little paranoia on my part, but I always make a point to lock all car doors when stepping out to fuel up.

Just in Case

Even though the vast majority of the time nothing will go wrong, there are always those few instances that can't be avoided. So just in case something does, keep these road trip safety tips in mind:

1. ALWAYS KEEP YOUR PHONE CHARGED

I make sure to check my phone's battery quite often and try to never let it dip below 40%. That way, in case anything does happen, I'm able to call for a tow truck or the police. Also, I can turn on my GPS if I don't know exactly where I'm at.

2. IN CASE OF A CAR BREAKDOWN: STAY CALM, TAKE A DEEP BREATH AND STAY PUT

As long as it is safe to do so, always remain in your vehicle until the police or the tow truck arrives. If someone does walk up to you to offer assistance, DO NOT OPEN YOUR DOOR. Instead, roll down the window just enough to talk to the individual but not enough that they can reach a hand inside. Even though it's very likely they are an honest person just trying to help, it's better to err on the side of caution, especially if you're traveling alone.

3. REMEMBER THERE'S SAFETY IN NUMBERS

If you ever feel uncomfortable or unsafe, head inside the nearest restaurant or crowded bar. Talk to the employees so someone knows you're there. If I'm ever traveling at night and have to stop, I like to find full-size truck stops because there are always plenty of lights, cameras all around the place, and there's always someone working inside. Plus, they usually don't mind if you hang out and chat for a bit until you're comfortable enough to get back on the road.

All in all, the best way to stay safe out on the road is to prepare, trust your instincts, and stay vigilant but not let the fear ruin your trip. Never forget that the reason you're out there is to enjoy the scenery, find inspiration, and search for the next best quilt shop!

QUILTY INSPIRATION AT THE SEATTLE AIRPORT

AIR TRAVEL SAFETY TIPS

With all the advancements in airport and airline security, I feel like many people have possibly been lulled into a false sense of safety in airports and on planes. It's almost as if once we walk through the TSA screening, all is well and we let down our guard. Unfortunately, that little paranoia button of mine never shuts off. So whether you're flying domestically or internationally, here are a few air travel safety tips I put together to help keep you on your toes.

Use TSA Locks On All Bags

Long gone are the days of simply zipping up your bags and heading to the airport. Sure, many people still do; however, with all the stories of belongings getting lost or bags thrown around, I find more a peace of mind by always using TSA-approved locks on all my bags, including my carry-ons. This way, no one can just open your bags while they're out of your sight, but TSA can still inspect the bags if necessary.

One major drawback for using these little TSA locks is their tiny little keys. I won't talk about how many suitcase keys have gone on travel adventures of their own, never to be seen again. However, I've since discovered an amazing tip for keeping them safe!

KEYCHAIN MINI QUILT

Now, you might be thinking, "Just put them on your keychain." But what if you're traveling alone and have to leave your keys with your spouse? Or your kids need the keychain because they're watching your house or taking care of your beloved pets? In this case, you'll need a sure-fire way to keep those tiny little buggers from wandering off.

Enter the mini quilt.

A couple years ago, I was gifted an adorable little mini quilt keychain. The "quilt" is completed like a pillowcase, with a pocket opening in the back. Inside, I store my little TSA lock keys and any other tiny objects I don't want to lose. The quilt pocket stays inside my travel purse and is always there when I need it.

Write Your Name And Phone Number Inside Your Checked Bag

If at all possible, I try not to check any baggage. However, in the instances when I must (like traveling internationally), I always write my name and phone number on a piece of paper and place it **inside** my luggage. The reason for this is twofold.

First, mostly I just don't trust those flimsy name tags they give you at the check-in counter. Secondly, because of advice from my sister who works for an airline at the Seattle airport. You'd be amazed at the number of bags that are lost and have no identification. When this happens, the first thing they do is open the bag to see if there is anything that will help identify the owner of the bag. Hence, the paper insert with name and phone number.

Protect Your Personal Information

At the TSA checkpoint, in order to get people through quickly, they ask that you have your boarding pass and ID at the ready. Have you ever looked at the people around you in line? Their personal ID information is readily available for anyone that wants to read it or worse, take a picture of it.

Therefore, instead of using paper boarding passes, I use the airline application on my cell phone. That way, all I have to do is bring it up on my phone as I approach the TSA agent. For my ID, I place it face-down on top of my phone. That way it's out and handy but all my personal information is covered.

Getting Through Screening

When you place your belongings on the conveyor belt for TSA screening, always place any electronics or your purse so they go through last. And, don't go through the metal detector until your belongings have entered the conveyor tunnel.

I've seen so many people take their laptops or phones out of their bags and leave them trailing behind as they go through the metal detector, open to the world in a tub on the counter. Yes, 99% of the time the people behind you will just push your bin forward. But there could be that one that just moves your device into their bin.

If possible, strike up a conversation with the person in front of you while waiting in line. That way, they'll be more apt to keep an eye out if your belongings come through before you do.

WAITING TO BOARD

Don't Get Rushed

When you're in line to get a bite to eat or grab something from the newsstand shop inside the airport, do you feel rushed by pretty much everyone around you? Me too. However, when we're rushed, we tend to forget little things. Things like grabbing your charge card back from the cashier (I've seen this happen more than once). Or if we pick things up too quickly, we drop them and don't even notice as we're running out to our gate.

Instead, I always try to make sure I have plenty of time before my flight boards, so I don't get rushed. When I make a purchase, I move my things over to the side of the counter and carefully put everything inside my bag before I leave the store/restaurant. This method reduces both stress and the chance that I'll forget something.

Don't Leave Your Bags

Ok, I know this one is harped on endlessly in messages to us from the airport personnel via the airport's PA system. However, we hear it so much now that we tend to tune it out. Don't leave your bags.

I was in Dallas waiting on a connecting flight when a girl, obviously traveling

LEFT–GUM WALL IN SEATTLE, TOP–FALL ON THE APPALACHIAN TRAIL, RIGHT–SOUTHEASTERN QUILT & TEXTILE MUSEUM

alone, set down her ear buds and her cell phone on top of her bag and got up to go throw away her garbage just as they began boarding. When she returned to her things, her phone was gone. Now, in this case, someone sitting nearby saw the stranger take the phone and spoke up, and the phone was returned. However, this crime victim got lucky. There have been too many times when people weren't so lucky.

As You Board Your Flight

Remember that "rushed" feeling? Yeah, it tends to kick into high gear when we're boarding. I'm not sure if it's more us putting pressure on ourselves or all the looks of the people around us, silently urging us to "Just sit down so we can go!" It's even worse when it's time to get OFF the plane. However, again, when we're rushed, we tend to forget things. Many, many things.

As I mentioned earlier, my sister works for an airline in Seattle, and we got to talking one day about all the things people have left behind on planes.

Everything from papers to phones to laptops. Yes, laptops. Honestly, who leaves a laptop on board a plane??

That wasn't even the worst. Once a woman left her wedding ring on board. I'm not kidding. My sister and the pilot spent entirely too long on hands and knees searching for this poor woman's ring. Luckily, they found it. But just imagine all the items that never get found. You think losing your luggage is bad. Imagine losing your phone.

Another tip I'd like to offer is about your overhead baggage. When possible, I try to not have any checked bags. Therefore, I pay a little extra for early boarding so I am guaranteed to have a good spot for my overhead bag. I like to keep it in the bin directly across from my seat so that I can keep an eye on it if someone opens the bin during flight. That may be a bit of overkill, but again, if you haven't noticed, I tend to err on the side of paranoia.

Pay Attention To The Safety Plan

I'll be honest, I've traveled so much in my life that I've seen hundreds, if not thousands, of those pre-flight safety plans the flight crew go through before each flight. I've seen them so much that I've found myself ignoring them altogether, because let's face it: If you've seen one, you've seen them all, right? Wrong.

Sitting here right now, I can probably only recite a couple of the items they go through from memory. For some reason the whole "Put the mask on yourself before your child" one has always stuck with me.

If I can't recite them all to you right now, I surely won't be able to remember them during an emergency. So no matter if you fly once a year or once a week, be sure to pay attention to the safety plan. It's better to be over-prepared than the reverse.

Make Sure Someone Has All Your Flight Information

Making sure someone knows your route is my #1 tip that I tell everyone. Mostly because you just never know what can happen. This is especially true when traveling alone.

Therefore, I like to make sure my husband or another family member or close friend has a copy of my entire itinerary, including all flight and hotel information, before I leave home. Also, I message the person I'm leaving and the person I'm going to see before each flight and as soon as we land. This helps keep people aware of your location and provides peace of mind for everyone involved.

Above all, traveling on an airplane can be a low-stress experience when you take a few precautions to help ease your mind.

TRAVELING POST-COVID

Let's face it. The world has changed. Long gone are the carefree days of blissfully walking through life, nary a thought to the thousands of germs we encounter every second of every day. No, sir. COVID has changed our world. Now germs are top of mind with every step we take: every trip to the grocery store and certainly every potential road trip or vacation we may plan.

To say things have gotten "a little out of hand" might be an understatement. However, before you start pouring hand sanitizer in places it doesn't need to go, here are my best safety tips for traveling in a post-COVID world to help quell your fears and inspire you to get back out on the road to your next quilt adventure!

Travel With Disinfecting Wipes

If you're like me, you travel with baby wipes. Yes, those time-tested cleaning sheets with the power of mom spit. The same ones our mothers (and possibly grandmothers) used to clean our behinds all the way through potty training.

Baby wipes are amazing little sheets. Seriously, after having my son I was truly amazed at the messes they were able to make disappear. However, as powerful as they are, baby wipes just don't hold up against COVID germs.

You see, baby wipes were designed to clean our rear ends. And, unfortunately, if they had the power to also "disinfect" (containing alcohol) we'd have surely given our children (and probably ourselves) a few hundred nasty rashes by now. So keep the baby wipes for our tears, ears, and rears and carry a few disinfecting wipes for everything else.

Baby Wipes = human skin

Disinfecting Wipes = Counters, tables, chairs and other surfaces our human skin may come in contact with.

✈ **PRO TIP:** *According to the EPA, 70% and above undiluted IPA (Isopropyl Alcohol), Ethanol (Ethyl Alcohol), or Hydrogen Peroxide will kill the Coronavirus.*

So, when adding disinfecting wipes to your travel kit, be sure to check the label and purchase ones that have at least 70% undiluted alcohol written on the label and specifically states the wipes are for "Disinfecting." However, only use them to clean surfaces according to their individual warning labels.

Wash Your Hands Often!

I heard a non-scientific radio program where they polled their audience, asking them for the number-one thing they will continue to do after the

NEON SIGN BONEYARD IN LAS VEGAS, NEVADA

pandemic dies down. Want to know what it was? No, it wasn't "working from home" or "Zoom calls," which would have been my top two guesses. Instead, it was "washing our hands."

You know the saying "Everything I need to know, I learned in kindergarten?" Well, this one holds true. To this day, the time-tested (and pediatrician approved) way to kill germs and stay safe is to simply wash your hands thoroughly. A good idea is to hum a verse from your favorite tune while digging those germ-killing soap particles into every single nook and crevice from your fingertips to your forearm. Seriously, you'd think I was preparing for surgery if you saw me washing my hands.

When you're out on the road and don't always have access to soap, you can use travel soap papers. These are actual soap that has been shaved down into small narrow strips resembling paper. I carry a pack of these little guys in all my travel kits. They're kind of awesome, compact, and you can use them with water from a sink, a bottle, or some other water you grab from a natural source.

Use This Cool Tool

In June 2020, my mom and I traveled to Las Vegas and stayed at the MGM Grand hotel. Waiting for us on the nightstand in our hotel room was a wonderful little bag of "health and safety goodies." Inside were two brand-new masks, a pen, hand sanitizer, and a nifty little metal thing. Admittedly, we had NO CLUE what that metal thing was or what it was used for. So, Mom put it in her purse and we went on our merry way.

NON-CONTACT DOOR OPENER

Flash forward a few weeks to when I stumbled upon an ad for that very same device and almost fell off my chair. That little metal thing is called a "non-contact door

opener and stylus." This thing is awesome! It hangs on your keychain, so you use it to touchlessly (is that a word?) open doors, push buttons, and even use public touch screens. That's right, all with no actual touching! Since Mom wouldn't give up the one we got from the MGM, I've since purchased a full set for myself and now I have them on sale in my own online store.

Travel Laundry Soap

When I go on my travels, sometimes I can be gone for a few weeks at a time. Obviously, I don't want to carry with me multiple weeks of different outfits, so I must do laundry. However, not all hotels or room shares have laundry facilities. This is the very reason I started carrying travel laundry soap. Plus, in the new

READY TO FLY!

world of COVID, I double-recommend traveling with them. Triple even. Here's why:

During the pandemic, I'd be willing to bet that you made a few (or more) cotton masks. I know some people literally made hundreds. Did you know that these cotton masks can possibly do more damage than good if you don't wash them after each use?

When you breathe out, the steam from your breath dampens the cotton mask just enough to potentially start collecting and breeding thousands of microscopic germs. The longer you use your mask without washing it, the higher your risk of infection. Obviously, I am not a doctor. However, a good friend of mine developed a staph infection on her face due to those nasty germs. Gross, right? So that's where the travel laundry soap comes in.

Travel laundry soap can be purchased in 3 forms:

- Tiny liquid pockets (Like pods)
- A nifty laundry soap bar
- And cool little laundry soap sheets similar to the hand soap sheets I mentioned previously.

No matter the package it comes in, each travel laundry soap can be used in the bathroom sink at your hotel or room share to wash your cotton masks. I suggest washing your masks every night in hot water and hanging them to dry overnight so they'll be fresh, clean and ready for the next day.

✈ **PRO TIP:** *If you are on a trip longer than a few days and don't want to take too many clothes, these travel laundry soaps are great for doing a bathroom sink full of laundry and hanging them in the shower or hotel room closet to dry overnight. If you do a Google or Amazon search, you can also find complete travel laundry kits that include a sink plug and clothesline.*

All in all, it's a brave new world my friend, and only the prepared will prosper. Or something like that. With a few basic precautions, not even germs can stop us from more amazing quilting adventures!

CHAPTER NINE

Quilt Projects on the Road

BEST PROJECTS TO TAKE ON THE ROAD

As I'm sure you've guessed by now, I love a great road trip. No matter if I'm traveling cross-country or across town to the next quilt shop, I'll take any excuse to get out for a new adventure. But for those longer journeys, it's good to have a project with me.

Driving from Reno to Las Vegas, Nevada, is approximately an 8-hour trip each direction. So, when Mom and I made the trip for her birthday, I wanted to take along a quilting project to help pass the time. I can't stand having idle hands. I'm fairly certain I get that from my grandmother.

Having a quilting project with you is great when you're traveling by air or by car, or even to take along on a quilt retreat for something to keep your hands busy during down time.

Here are my top 5 quilting projects you can sew on the road.

IN-FLIGHT EPP

1. English Paper Piecing (EPP)

English Paper Piecing is the art of wrapping fabric around a paper template (usually in hexagons and other geometric shapes) and then stitching them together to form your quilt top.

EPP is my "go-to" project when I'm traveling because you can take it almost anywhere. In fact, all of the required tools (precut fabric, templates, small snips, thread, and a small tube of glue) will fit inside your purse or handbag. Then, whether you're on a 6-hour plane ride across the Atlantic Ocean or enduring a 30-minute wait for a quilt show to begin, you have something at the ready to keep your hands busy.

2. Hooped Embroidery

Hooped embroidery is the art of stitching thread designs into fabric using an embroidery hoop to stabilize the fabric. These projects can include everything from monogramming to applique to counted cross stitch and more.

When I was a teenager, cross stitch was the first sewing technique I learned to make. Today, I use my embroidery hoop for many different projects, including counted cross stitch. Just like EPP, hooped embroidery is an excellent project to take with you on the road as it is portable and all the needed supplies don't take up too much room in your bag.

That said, it all depends on the size of your hoop. If you use a larger-sized hoop, or floor stand hoop, this obviously won't work well in a car or on a plane. However, if you stick to a smaller-sized hoop (12-inch diameter and under) you should be good to go.

3. Hand Applique

The hand applique technique is the process of hand stitching one small piece of fabric on top of another larger piece of fabric. Recently I have been getting more and more into hand applique. Once you get the hang of the process, you can use it to create some incredibly unique designs.

Hand applique is also a great road trip project because, like the hooped embroidery, it can be done using a wood or plastic hoop. Just remember to keep the hoop size under 12 inches so it will store easily in your carry-on bag.

✈ **PRO TIP:** *When I take an applique project with me on the road, I like to spray baste my applique pieces to the foundation fabric before I leave. Alternatively, you can use double-sided fusible interfacing to adhere the fabrics together. This saves time, doesn't require a lot of pins, and prevents the fabric pieces from moving around while traveling.*

4. Hand Quilting

The time-honored tradition of hand quilting your quilt sandwich is perfect for traveling in a car or on an airplane. It is especially great if you're like me and have a tendency to freeze wherever you go. I swear my husband keeps the

car at 60 degrees just to annoy me.

The overall size of your quilt will depend on where you can easily work on them. For instance, a throw, baby quilt, or lap-size quilt is great for hand quilting on an airplane. However, the full, queen, and king sizes should probably be reserved for working on in a car as they take up much more room and would be harder to fit inside your carry-on baggage.

Also, keep in mind your hoop size and basting technique. If you use a quilting hoop, be sure to keep it under 12 inches for easier transport. Also, if you spray baste your quilt sandwich, you shouldn't have any issues. If you pin baste your quilts, keep in mind it may cause some questioning by the TSA. The risk of any real issues is very, very small. However, ultimately, what is and isn't allowed through the TSA security checkpoints is up to the TSA agents on duty.

5. Hand Binding a Quilt

Just like hand quilting, hand binding your quilt is another great project for both road and air travel. While I am a machine binder, I do know of a few fabric and pattern designers that have had to do last-minute hand binding for a quilt sample on the plane as they travel to their next quilt show!

When hand binding a quilt, the same "rules" apply as with hand quilting. If you use a hoop, make sure your hoop size is small enough to fit inside your carry-on for air travel and keep in mind what sort of pinning you use to apply your binding. Again, having lots and lots of pins may cause some questions at TSA checkpoints. To avoid any issues, I suggest using those fabulous binding clips we see in all the quilt stores these days. I use them for so many things, not just binding.

No matter where your destination or how long it takes to get there, having a great quilt project to take along helps the time go faster, and you'll soon have a fabulous new quilt!

WHAT QUILTING SUPPLIES CAN YOU TAKE ON AN AIRPLANE?

I fly quite a bit. In fact, I've been flying an average of once a year since I was 6 months old. Therefore, I try to stay up-to-date on the ins and outs of Travel Safety Association (TSA) regulations and which quilting supplies you can and cannot take on board an airplane.

While most things are pretty obvious, we quilters have a unique set of supplies. You might be surprised at some of the supplies that are actually allowed on board an aircraft. Keep in mind the final decision is ultimately up to the discretion of the TSA agents at each airport. So it's a good idea to bring a self-addressed stamped envelope with you, just in case. I learned that lesson the hard way.

GAVIN AT A CAR MUSEUM IN TACOMA, WASHINGTON

A few years back, my son and I were flying home from San Francisco. On the flight there, he packed his lucky pocket knife inside his checked bag. No problems. However, for the flight home, he conveniently forgot he had moved to knife into his carry-on backpack. Of course, the TSA found it.

Luckily for my son, the airport had a mail drop off service. Even though the postage cost me $35, we were still able to mail the knife home so that we didn't lose it. Oh, was my son surprised when he learned of all the extra chores he had to do to pay me back!

SOMETHING TO KEEP YOU BUSY

If you want to bring a fun quilting project to keep you busy on your flight and/or airport layover, you can bring all of the following quilting supplies on board the airplane:

Fabric

Hand quilting projects are always great to take on a plane. And obviously there's no problem taking the fabric on board. However, make sure all your fabric pieces are precut before you leave home as you will not be able to bring your large fabric scissors on board.

✈ **PRO TIP:** *Make sure to bring more pieces than you think you'll need. After all, it's better to have too much than too little!*

Sewing Needle & Thread

You can definitely take sewing needles on board an aircraft. However, I highly suggest keeping them pushed into a pincushion with a piece of thread attached through the needle's eye. That way, there's less chance of them getting bent or broken.

Scissors

The TSA does allow scissors on board an aircraft if the blades are smaller than 4 inches. However, it is still ultimately up to the individual agent's discretion, so don't bring your favorite pair. I like to bring a cheap pair of dollar store snips on flights and leave my favorite Karen Kay Buckley's at home.

✈ **PRO TIP:** *In a pinch, some good alternatives to scissors are small nail clippers or even a dental floss container. You can also bring precut thread.*

Other Items

Other items you should have no problem bringing on board an aircraft are paper templates (precut) for English paper piecing, small embroidery hoops, as well as knitting and crochet needles for our multi-crafting friends.

BUT I NEED EVERYTHING!

If you're travel destination is a quilt retreat or a large quilt show where you'll need most of your quilting supplies, did you know that you CAN take your sewing machine on board an airplane? It's true! However, there are a couple things to keep in mind.

When traveling with your sewing machine, it needs to fit under the seat in front of you, so make sure you're not bringing a big heavy machine. If you can, bring a smaller travel-size machine that has a suitcase or carrying case. I travel with my Brother machine workhorse that I've had for ages. It has its own travel case and travels very well.

Just to avoid any issues with the TSA, I take the needle out of my machine and store it with my other supplies in my checked baggage. Also, you may want to add a little extra time going through TSA security as they will more than likely want to take the machine out of its case for inspection.

Items to Pack in Your Checked Baggage

Here is a short list of things you should definitely place in your **checked** baggage:

- **All blades longer than 4 inches:** This includes your rotary cutter and fabric scissors. You cannot take either of them on board, but you can check them with no problems.
- **Seam ripper:** Because of their pointed ends, seam rippers are a no-go for on board travel. I don't really get it, either. However, just to be safe, you're better off tucking them safely away in your checked baggage.
- **Cutting mat:** First and foremost, make sure you have a suitcase large enough to lay your cutting mat flat so that it doesn't get warped during the flight. That is the reason I usually don't travel with my big 18 x 24 cutting mat unless I know I'll really need it.
- **Iron:** You can definitely pack your iron in your checked baggage. However, to save space, I like to travel with my little craft-size iron when necessary. Most quilt retreats and quilt show classes will provide irons for you to use. But I like to have my little one just in case I want to work on a project in my room at night.

If you're ever concerned about what items you can or can't take on an airplane, you can always contact the TSA and/or the airports you'll be traveling from. Don't forget to check your return flight airport!

Apart from the TSA, each airport and each individual airline may have their own rules regarding what quilting items you can and can't take on board an airplane. If you call them, be sure to write down who you talked to and when just in case a security agent questions you at airport security.

No matter where you're flying or for what purpose, the most important thing is to stay safe, be creative, and have fun! Every moment can be a grand adventure!

BONUS CHAPTER

Quilt Patterns

As I mentioned at the beginning of this book, I had put together a group of quilts that were inspired by our Quilt Tour to Ireland in 2017. Since that book did not transpire, I decided to add in 3 of them here for you to enjoy!

RAINBOWS ON THE OCEAN

FINISHED SIZE: 48" X 60"

As we were traveling throughout Ireland we saw a rainbow nearly every day. Rainbows of all sizes and brightness. Now, I know the appearance of rainbows is purely scientific due to the light being reflected off of the clouds, etc. However, the believer in me likes to see them as Ireland itself was blessing our journey.

Combine all those rainbows with the fact that Ireland is in fact an island surrounded by water and you have my thought process for Rainbows on the Ocean.

MATERIALS REQUIRED

Various Blues	4¼ yds
Red	¼ yd
Orange	¼ yd
Yellow	¼ yd
Green	¼ yd
Purple	¼ yd
Binding Fabric	½ yd
Backing Fabric	3 yds
Batting	56" x 68"

PATTERN NOTES:

- Skill Level: Beginner
- Yardage based on 42" width of fabric.
- All fabric quantities rounded up to nearest ¼ yd.
- Seams are a scant ¼" unless otherwise stated.
- WOF = Width of Fabric
- RST = Right Sides Together

CUTTING

Choose your quilt size and cut pieces according to the lists below. All instructions on this pattern are based on the Wall/Lap size quilt design.

QUANTITY	SIZE
Red Scraps	
2	9" x 2½" (J)
4	10½" x 2" (K)
2	10½" x 1" (L)
2	12½" x 2½" (M)
Orange Scraps	
2	10½" x 2" (K)
3	10½" x 1" (L)
3	12½" x 2½" (M)
Yellow Scraps	
1	3½" x 3½" (A)
1	4" x 2" (C)
1	8½" x 2½" (I)
3	9" x 2½" (J)
2	10½" x 2" (K)
1	12½" x 2½" (M)
Green Scraps	
1	4" x 2" (C)
2	6" x 2" (E)
2	6½" x 2" (F)
1	7½" x 1" (G)
3	7" x 1½" (H)
3	8½" x 2½" (I)
2	10½" x 2" (K)
1	10½ " x 1" (L)
1	12½" x 2½" (M)

QUANTITY	SIZE
Blue Scraps	
15	3½" x 3½" (A)
16	3½" x 1" (B)
16	4" x 2" (C)
19	5" x 2½" (D)
17	6" x 2" (E)
17	6½" x 2" (F)
18	7½" x 1" (G)
17	7" x 1½" (H)
15	8½" x 2½" (I)
15	9" x 2½" (J)
29	10½" x 2" (K)
14	10½" x 1" (L)
12	12½" x 2½" (M)
Purple Scraps	
4	3½" x 3½" (A)
4	3½" x 1" (B)
2	4" x 2" (C)
1	5" x 2½" (D)
1	6" x 2" (E)
1	6½" x 2" (F)
1	7½" x 1" (G)
1	8½" x 2½" (I)
1	10½" x 2" (K)
1	12½" x 2½" (M)

BLOCK CONSTRUCTION

Blue Log Cabin Blocks

1. Using random blue pieces, stitch one 3½" x 3½" (A) blue square with one 1" x 3½" (B) blue strip, RST. Press seam open.

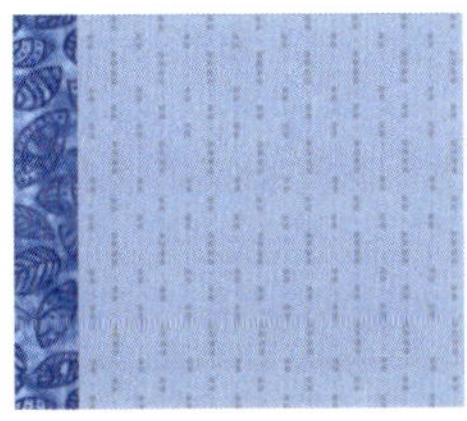

2. Stitch one 2" x 4" (C) blue piece to the Right side of the A/B unit, as shown, RST. Press seam open.

3. Stitch one (D) 2½" x 5" blue piece to the bottom of your unit, as shown, RST. Press seam open.

4. Stitch one (E) 2" x 6" blue piece to the Right side of your unit, as shown, RST. Press seam open.

5. Stitch one (F) 2" x 6½" blue piece to the bottom of your unit, as shown, RST. Press seam open.

6. Stitch one (G) 1" x 7 ½" blue piece to the Right side of your unit, as shown, RST. Press seam open.

7. Stitch one (H) 1½" x 7" blue piece to the bottom of your unit, as shown, RST. Press seam open.

8. Stitch one (I) 2½" x 8½" blue piece to the Right side of your unit, as shown, RST. Press seam open.

9. Stitch one (J) 2½" x 9" blue piece to the bottom of your unit, as shown, RST. Press seam open.

10. Stitch one (K) 2" x 10½" piece to the Right side of your unit, as shown, RST. Press seam open.

11. Stitch one (L) 1" x 10½" blue piece to the bottom of your unit, as shown, RST. Press seam open.

12. Stitch one (M) 2" x 10½" blue piece to the Right side of your unit, as shown, RST. Press seam open.

13. Stitch one (N) 2½" x 12½" blue piece to the bottom of your unit, as shown, RST. Press seam open.

14. Repeat steps 1 – 13 using all random blue pieces to make a total of 8 Blue Log Cabin Blocks.

Trim blocks to 12½" x 12½" unfinished.

Rainbow Log Cabin Blocks

1. Using the Rainbows on the Ocean quilt layout below as a fabric color guide, repeat steps 1 – 13 to complete Blocks 5 – 16.

ASSEMBLY

1. Stitch together into rows as shown. Press all seams open.

40 SHADES OF GREEN

FINISHED SIZE: 51" X 64"

Out in the western part of Ireland there is a popular pull over spot as you make your way out to the Wild Atlantic Way. This particular location made the cost of the entire trip worth every penny. As you look across the vast hillside you truly understand why Johnny Cash wrote the song, "40 Shades of Green."

Combine that with those amazing short rock walls and you get my 40 Shades quilt.

MATERIALS REQUIRED

Various Scraps	Varied
Sashing	½ yd
Corner Stones	¼ yd
Binding	½ yd
Backing	4 yds
Batting	Twin

PATTERN NOTES:

- Skill Level: Beginner
- Yardage based on 42" width of fabric.
- All fabric quantities rounded up to nearest ¼ yd.
- Seams are a scant ¼" unless otherwise stated.
- WOF = Width of Fabric
- RST = Right Sides Together

CUTTING

The blocks in this quilt will use a TON of your scraps. Cut the sashing and corner stones according to the list below.

	QUANTITY	SIZE
Sashing	31	1½" x 12½"
Corner Stones	12	1½" x 1½"

BLOCK CONSTRUCTION

1. ORGANIZE YOUR SCRAPS

Gather as many scraps as you can, then add some more. Every time I've made scrappy crazy blocks, I've always ended up a few scraps short.

Once you have all your fabrics together, I suggest organizing them by color or hue. For this quilt, all my scraps are organized by shade of green.

2. CHOOSE 2 SCRAPS

To get the best look for your crazy block, choose 2 fabrics that are of contrasting shades. For instance, a light fabric with a dark fabric.

3. TRIM AND STITCH

Place your 2 scraps RST and line up the edges as close as possible. Next, use your ruler and rotary cutter to trim both fabrics and create a straight edge.

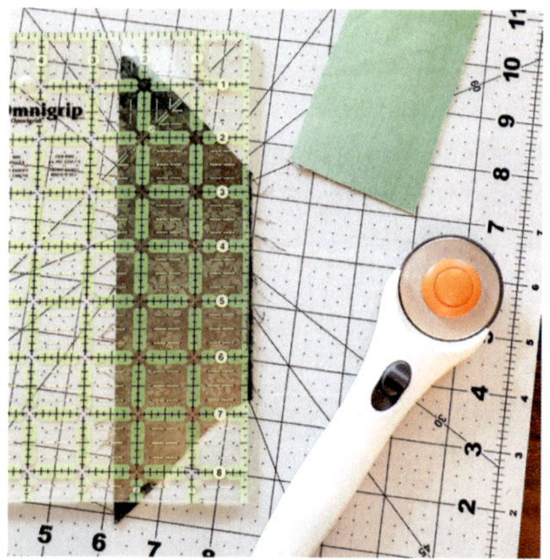

Pin them in place.

Stitch your ¼" seam along your straight edge. Press your seam open.

4. ADD FABRIC NUMBER THREE

Grab your next scrap. This time I suggest using a neutral or mid-range color/shade.

Using your ruler and rotary cutter again, trim one edge of both your Crazy Block Unit and your fabric number three.

Line up the straight edges, as shown, and stitch. Press this seam toward fabric number three.

5. JUST KEEP ADDING FABRIC

Using the directions in Step 4, keep adding scrap pieces until your block is slightly bigger than your 12½" x 12½" square ruler.

6. TRIM YOUR BLOCK

Once you have your scraps together, center your 12½" x 12½" square ruler over your block and trip around the edges.

7. RINSE AND REPEAT

Repeat steps 2 – 6 to complete a total of 20 crazy quilt blocks.

SASHING STRIPS

1. Place one 1½" x 1½" Cornerstone square on the end of one 1½" x 12½" sashing strip, RST. Press toward the sashing strip.

2. Place one 1½" x 1½" Cornerstone square on the opposite end of your sashing strip, RST. Press toward the sashing strip.

3. Continue adding 1½" x 1½" Cornerstones (C.S.) and 1½" x 12½" sashing strips to complete one full sashing row.

4. Repeat steps 15 – 17 to complete a total of FOUR Sashing Strip Rows.

ASSEMBLY

1. Stitch together your rows as shown. Press all seams toward the sashing.

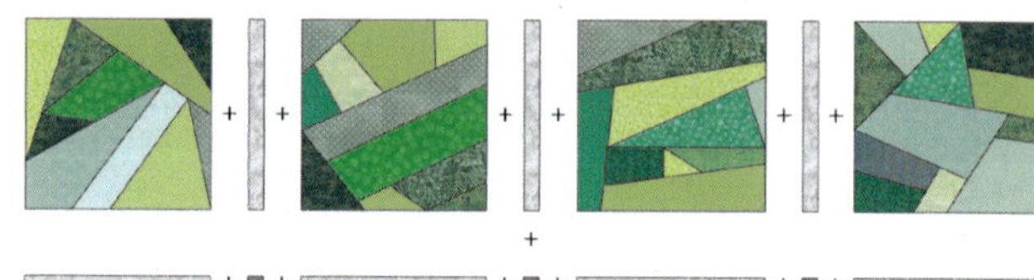

FINISHING

2. Sandwich and baste your Backing, Batting and Quilt top. Quilt as desired and Bind.From Grocery Shopping To Road Trip Packing To Quilt Retreats, This Bag Fits Them All! So far I've made three of these fabulous tote bags and will probably end up making at least three more. They have a super strong base that will hold a ton of weight. In fact, I've filled them up with cans and jars at the grocery store with no problems. Planning a road trip? This is your tote bag! Everything you need to keep in the car can be held inside these great bags.

ROCK WALLS IN WESTERN IRELAND

Omnigrip

ROAD TRIP TOTE BAG

DIMENSIONS: 15″ X 12″ X 8″

Heading for a quilt retreat or quilt class? This is your tote bag! It will hold all of your supplies including these 12" x 12" plastic project boxes! Seriously, I have a TON of these boxes for my projects. Each one holds your 12" x 12" inch quilt blocks perfectly! This overall pattern is pretty simple to follow even if you've never made a bag before.

MATERIALS REQUIRED

- Main Fabric – ½ yard (Bag outside)
- Lining Fabric – 1¼ yard (Bag inside and Outside Pockets)
- Contrast Fabric 1¼ yard (Handles and Bag bottom)
- Pellon 50 Fusible Heavyweight Interfacing – 1½ yards (20" wide)
- Coordinating Thread. I used Aurifil 50 wt. Black and Grey threads.

✈ PATTERN NOTES:

- Skill Level: Beginner
- Yardage based on 42″ width of fabric.
- *All seams are ½″.
- WOF = Width of Fabric
- RST = Right Sides Together

CUTTING

MAIN FABRIC:

- Outside Body – 20" x 15" (x2)

LINING FABRIC:

- 20" x 40" (x1)
- Outside Pockets – 8" x 18" (x2)

CONTRAST FABRIC:

- Handles – 4" x 48" (x2)
- Outside Base – 20" x 12" (x1)

FUSIBLE HEAVYWEIGHT INTERFACING:

- 20" x 15" (x2)
- 8" x 9" (x2)
- 20" x 12" (x1)

CONSTRUCTION

Applying Interfacing

1. Following the directions for the fusible interfacing, fuse together one 20" x 15" fusible interfacing piece to the WRONG side of each 20" x 15" Outside Body fabric pieces.

2. Fuse one each 8" x 9" fusible interfacing to half of the WRONG side of each 8" x 18" Outside Pocket pieces.

3. Fold each Outside Pocket piece in half, WRONG sides together.

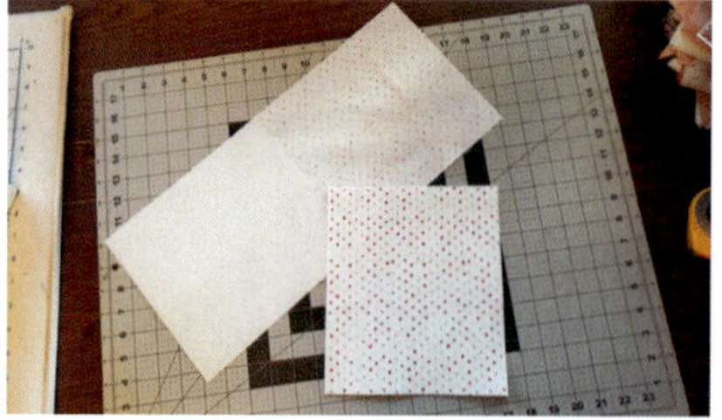

4. Fuse the 20" x 12" Interfacing to the WRONG side of Bag Bottom Piece.

Handles

1. Fold each 4" x 48" Handle piece lengthwise, WRONG sides together and press.

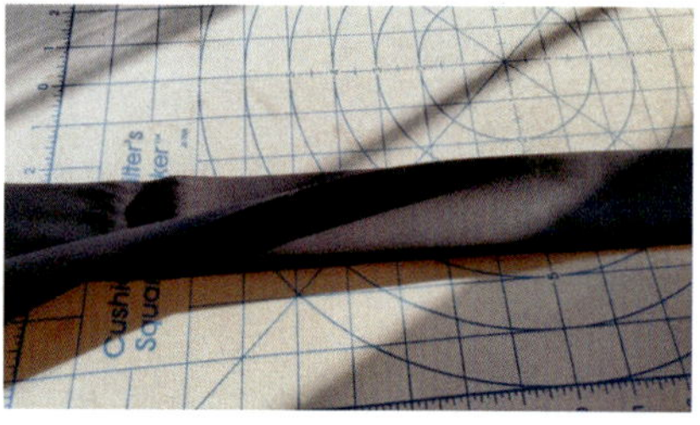

2. Open the Handle piece and fold each side toward the middle lengthwise and press.

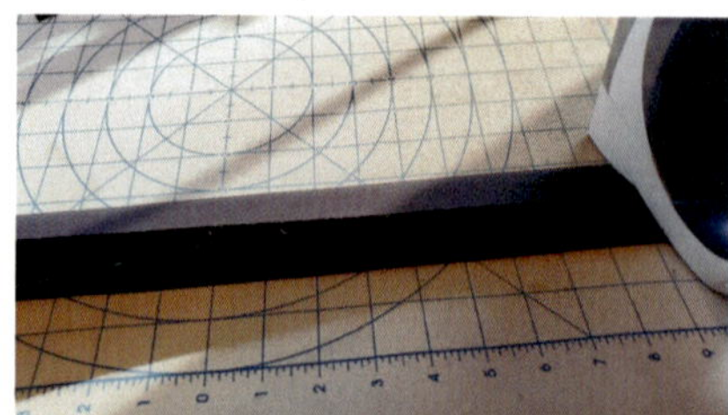

3. Fold the Handle piece in the center again creating a Double Fold. Press firmly.

4. Stitch along both sides of the Handle, lengthwise. Repeat with second Handle piece.

Outside Bag Body

1. Line up one pocket with the raw edges of the Outside body centers. Lay one Handle so the sides cover the side edges of the pocket. Line up all the raw edges at the bottom of each piece as shown. Pin in place.

2. Measure 1 inch from the top of the bag on the Handle piece as shown. This will make room to stitch the Lining and Bag Body together later.

3. Stitch each side of the Handles in place and across your drawn line at the top.

** Be sure to leave that 1 inch open from the top of the Outside Body pieces.*

4. Repeat with second Outside body piece, Handle and Outside Pocket. Place raw edges of Outside Base piece and one Outside Body piece, RIGHT sides together. Stitch along the bottom raw edges.

5. Press toward the Outside Base. Topstitch along seam.

6. Repeat with second Outside Body piece and opposite raw edge of Outside Base.

7. Press toward Base and Topstitch along seam.

8. Fold the full Outside Body in half, RIGHT sides together. Stitch along each side.

Box Your Corners

1. Fold one corner in to make a triangle. Measure 3½" up from the corner point at the seam. Side to side should measure 7". Draw a line across corner. Stitch ON your drawn line.

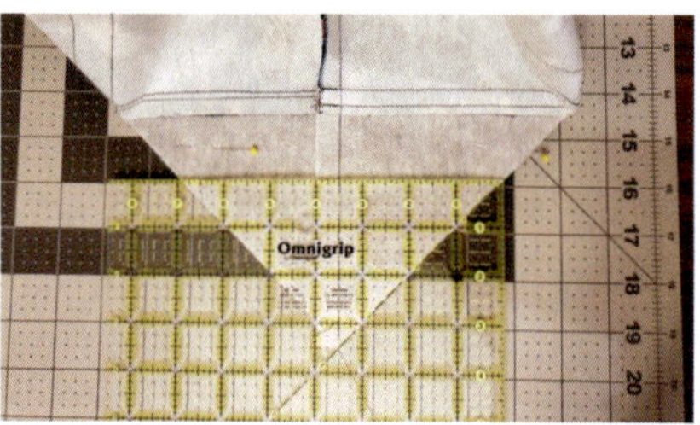

2. Fold stitched corner UP so that it lays flat against the Body side. Stitch to the side of the Outside Body. Repeat with second corner of Outside Body.

3. Turn Body RIGHT Side Out and set aside.

Lining

1. Fold 20" x 40" Lining fabric piece in half, RIGHT sides together to make a 20" x 20" piece. Stitch along each side, leaving approximately 6" OPEN on one side for turning.

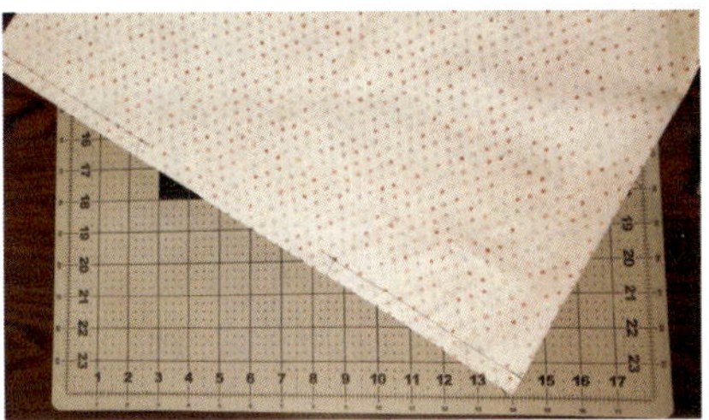

2. Box the corners the same as you did with the Outside Bag Body pieces. Measure 3½" UP. Stitch on drawn line.

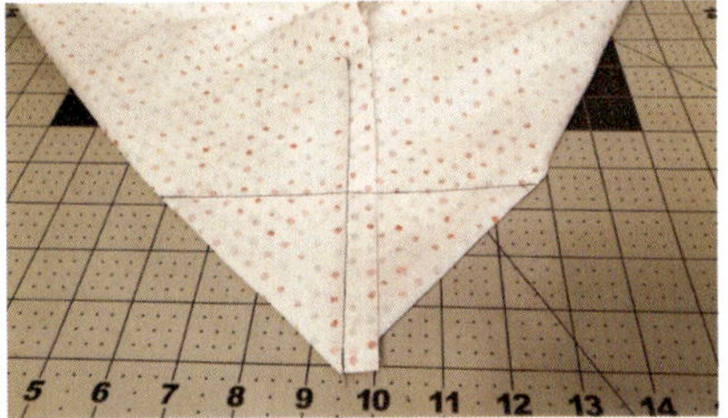

3. Fold UP and stitch to the side of the Bag Lining. Repeat with second corner of the Bag Lining.

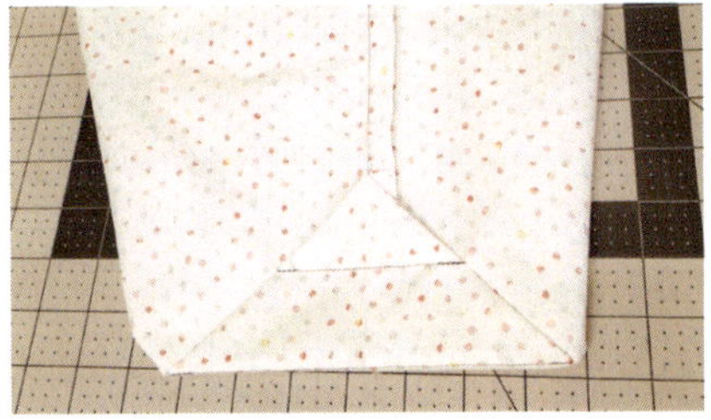

FINISHING

1. Place the Outside Bag INSIDE the Bag Lining. They should be RIGHT sides together. Line up the Side Seams and pin around the Top Edges. Make sure the Handles are tucked inside and free from the seam! Stitch around the entire Top Edge.

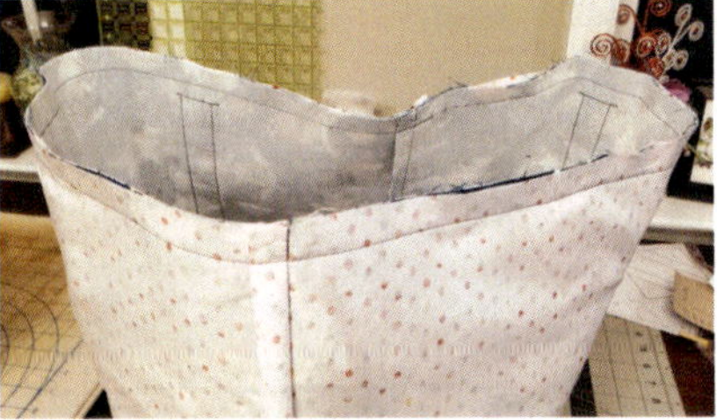

2. Pull the Bag RIGHT side out through the opening in the Lining.

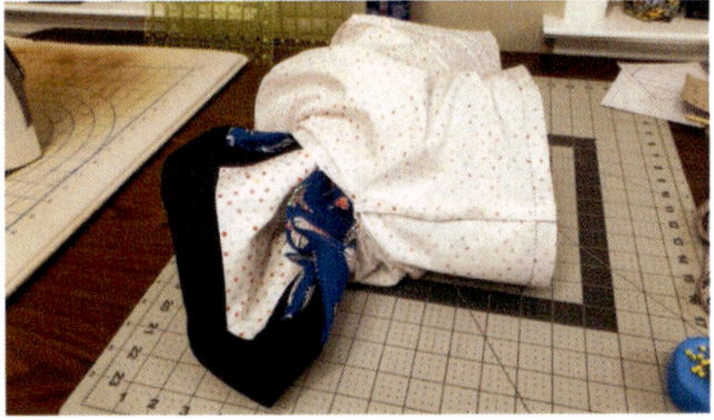

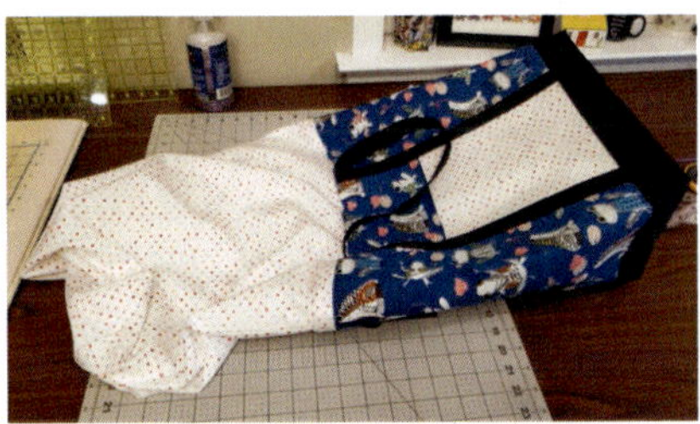

3. Stitch Lining opening closed.

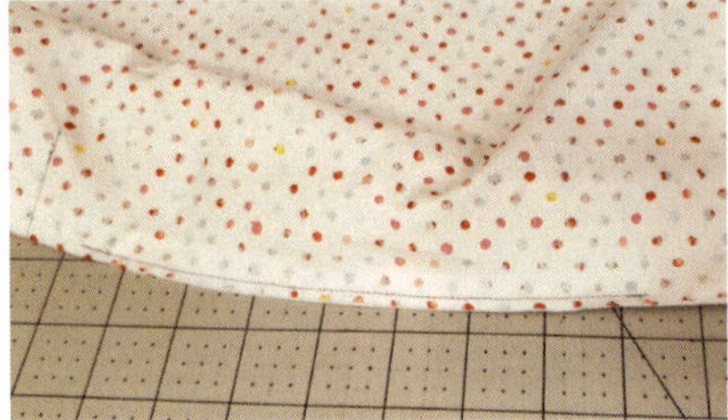

4. Tuck the Lining back inside the Bag. Press top edges firmly. Top Stitch around then entire Bag Top.

That's it! Now you're ready to use your amazing All Purpose Tote Bag! From grocery shopping to Road Tripping to Quilt Shows and Retreats, this great basic bag is the perfect all purpose tote bag you'll need!

Resources

SUGGESTED WEBSITES

AirBnB.com	Homestay website
JoinHoney.com	Automatic Couponing site
RetailMeNot.com	Coupons and other savings website
Groupon.com	Coupon website
Allianz.com	Travel Insurance company
AAA.com	American Automobile Association, federation of motor clubs
US.Norton.com	Norton online security company
TaxFoundation.org	Independent Tax Policy 501(c)3 nonprofit, Global tax statistics
X-rates.com	Global exchange rates and currency calculator
Amazon.com	Global shopping site
Signal.org	Global independent cell phone communication application
GoogleMaps.com	Online map site
Furkot.com	Online map site
RoadTrippers.com	Online map site
AtlasObscured.com	Online guide book for little known travel destinations
TheCultureTrip.com	Travel site
VisitNC.com	North Carolina travel site
BarnQuiltInfo.com	Online search for Barn quilt maps
QuiltTrailsWNC.org	Barn Quilt trail maps for North Carolina

PERSONALITIES

Rick Steves
RickSteves.com .... pgs. 6, 16
Facebook.com/ricksteves
Instagram.com/rickstevesEurope

Dave Ramsey
RamseySolutions.com .... p. 14
Facebook.com/daveramsey
Instagram.com/daveramsey

Cindy Lohbeck HandsonHandDyes.com .... pg. 32
Facebook.com/HandsOnHandDyes
Instagram.com/dyehardinaz

Kimberly Einmo KimberlyEinmo.com .... pg. 42
Facebook.com/kimberlyeinmodesigns
Instagram.com/kimberlyeinmodesigns

Beverly Y. Smith BeverlyYSmithArt.com .... pg. 42
Instagram.com/quiltbev

Christa Watson Christaquilts.com .... pg. 42
Facebook.com/Christa-Quilts-Inc-114868936875629
Instagram.com/christaquilts

Kaffe Fassett KaffeFassett.com .... pg. 42
Facebook.com/kaffefassettstudio
Instagram.com/kaffefassettstudio

Brandon Mably BrandonMably.com .... pg. 42
Facebook.com/brandonmablydesigns
Instagram.com/brandonmably

Ricky Tims RickyTims.com .... pg. 42
Facebook.com/RickyTims
Instagram.com/rickytims

Mark Sherman RemarkableQuilts.com .... pg. 73
Facebook.com/remarkablequiltsmarksherman
Instagram.com/remarkablequiltsbymark

QUILT SHOPS AND OTHER STORES

THE COTTON QUILT SHOP

4900 Troy Road, Granite Falls, NC 28630
828-244-7797
TheCottonQuilt.com

QUILT-N-CODE QUILT SHOP
208 East-West Blvd, #1A, Burnsville, NC 28714
828-536-5400
Quilt-N-Code.com

STITCHIN' HEAVEN
StitchinHeaven.com

FROND FABRICS
FrondDesignStudios.com

THIMBLES FOR YOU
ThimblesForYou.com

OFF THE WALL QUILT
OffTheWallQuilt.com

MISSOURI STAR QUILT COMPANY
VisitMSQC.com
MissouriStarQuiltCo.com

QUILT SHOWS

QUILT MARKET AND INTERNATIONAL QUILT FESTIVAL
Quilts.com

ORIGINAL SEWING & QUILT EXPO (OSQE)
SewingExpo.com

QUILTCON
QuiltCon.com

MID-ATLANTIC QUILT FESTIVAL
QuiltFest.com

QUILT RETREAT CENTERS

PONDEROSA QUILT RETREAT CENTER

184 Park Drive, Waynesville, NC 28786
704-682-9567
SummitQuiltRetreat.com

QUILT TOUR COMPANIES

CRAFT TOURS

815-663-4046
CraftTours.com

QUILT AND CRUISE

302-530-6187
QuiltandCruise.com

US QUILT TOURS

864-263-7962
USQuiltTours.com

OTHER MENTIONS

QUILT! CAROLINA SHOP HOP

QuiltCarolina.com

CHARLOTTE QUILTERS GUILD

CharlotteQuiltersGuild.org

MODERN QUILT GUILD

TheModernQuiltGuild.com

MANZANAR HISTORIC SITE

Manzanar Reward Road, California
NPS.gov/manz

HERMITAGE MUSEUM
7637 N Shore Road, Norfolk, VA 23505
TheHermitageMuseum.org

WEST ROWAN FARM, HOME AND GARDEN
11575 NC-801, Mt Ulla, NC 28125
704-278-2800
WestRowanBarnQuilts.com

ONE OF A KIND ART GALLERY
90 Cherokee Road, Pinehurst, NC 28374
910-725-0465
OOAKArtGallery.com

CROSSNORE WEAVERS
828-733-4660
Crossnore.org

HICKORY RIDGE LIVING HISTORY MUSEUM
591 Horn in the West Drive, Boone, NC 28607
HornInTheWest.com/museum

AVOCA WOOLEN MILLS
Avoca.com

Afterword

At the end of the day, no matter which quilt travel adventure you choose, the best reason to step out of your normal day-to-day routine is fellowship. Quilters are truly a unique breed. We are a creative, talented, unique, fun-loving, crazy, fun group of people. We come in all different ages, colors, shapes, and sizes. But at our core, we all have one big thing in common: a fabric addiction. That, and our love of the art of quilting. Our passion to create drives us to our next masterpiece. And our love of adventure can drive us to our next best friends. We truly are a gigantic, worldwide, one-of-a-kind community.

Are you ready to get out there and see just how big our world really is?